NEW DECORATIONS WITH

PODS, CONES, AND LEAVES

OTHER BOOKS BY ELEANOR VAN RENSSELAER

Decorating with Pods and Cones   1957

*Decorating with Seed Mosaics, Chipped Glass,
and Plant Materials*   1960

New Decorations with

PODS, CONES, AND LEAVES

ELEANOR VAN RENSSELAER

PHOTOGRAPHS BY DOUG MORRIS

D. VAN NOSTRAND COMPANY, INC.

Princeton, New Jersey

Toronto   *New York*   *London*

D. VAN NOSTRAND COMPANY, INC.
120 Alexander St., Princeton, New Jersey *(Principal office)*
24 West 40 Street, New York 18, New York

D. VAN NOSTRAND COMPANY, LTD.
358 Kensington High Street, London, W.14, England

D. VAN NOSTRAND COMPANY (Canada), LTD.
25 Hollinger Road, Toronto 16, Canada

Published simultaneously in Canada by
D. VAN NOSTRAND COMPANY (Canada), LTD.

Library of Congress Catalog Card No. 66-27526

PRINTED IN THE UNITED STATES OF AMERICA

To my gifted associates who studied with me

at Villa Montalvo in Saratoga, California.

Their ingenuity and imagination have been a

continuing inspiration throughout the past decade.

MY THANKS

To those talented members of my classes whose designs appear in this book.

To Cynthia C. Luden whose painstaking editorial work has contributed to the clarity of my text.

Foreword

The years have added up to a quarter of a century since I first became fascinated with natural forms in all stages of development from the flower to the final berry, fruit, seed pod, or cone. From seeing plants as a whole I became aware of their individual parts. On the ground under tree or shrub, I often found interesting pieces cast off at some time through the year; now month by month I watch for these developments. And I observe the stages flowers pass through in gardens and how weeds mature along the roadside.

When I first began to work with these materials, they were rarely used except that cones were added to green Christmas wreaths. Now dried things interest almost all flower arrangers, and no show is complete without a section for these permanent decorations.

At the start of my collecting there were no dealers in dried flowers, pods, and cones. Now there are many, both wholesale and retail. When Styrofoam was introduced for Christmas decorations, I tried to find cone shapes for tree designs, but not until the 1950's were wreath frames and tapered forms available. With these, fresh possibilities were opened up for amateur and professional decorators. New glues and adhesives came on the market, and teachers of decorative arts learned how to use resin to produce sparkling and unusual creations. In *Decorating with Seed Mosaics, Chipped Glass, and Plant Materials,* I told how to heat and crackle broken glass, and these pieces embedded in plastic or combined with natural materials offer more colorful possibilities.

I live in a rather leisurely place where much fine craft work is produced and appreciated. Many classes are conducted in cultural centers and there are a number of adult educational projects. It is almost impossible to keep up with all the stimulating lecture programs dealing with the creative use of natural materials. What a wholesome trend this is—nature appreciated by people of all ages. What a satisfying development I have shared.

Once you discover the fascination of collecting new forms of plant life, you will surely fall under the spell of the great range of nature; you will be forever gathering rocks, pebbles, shells, and driftwood just as I do. My storage areas contain boxes and baskets filled with treasures from beaches and mountains as well as from gardens and fields. And now that I am making designs for outdoor living on patios and sundecks that require screens and textural fencing, I find that I need a great deal of material. Sometimes gardens are built around rocks, and for these there are also outdoor decorations. I have therefore included a chapter with ideas for enhancing patio walls or making screens to separate the parts of a garden. Since natural materials need protection from weather I coat them with plastic, pouring it on in small quantities over the whole decoration, or I apply one of the other protective finishes suggested in the text.

Some of my most exotic and colorful pods and cones, which are pictured and identified in this book, have come from a dealer who collected them in Australia, New Zealand, and South Africa for her own use in making arrangements and for kits to be marketed. These unusual items are now available to you by mail. (See "Sources of Supplies.")

A design with natural materials should be created with a feeling for its appropriate use, its relationship and proportionate size to the area in which it will be displayed and lighted. The principles of design that apply to any art form also apply to work with natural materials. The ability to do creative work can certainly be developed with practice; skill with the hands may

perhaps be God-given, but this too can be improved
with effort. Once the mind is awakened to awareness of
forms, large and small, in nature, a new world is
revealed.

When you are designing, you will discover that you
can combine these forms and that the design you con-
template can be evolved in more than one way. Try to
visualize objects not as a whole but instead concentrate
on the lines they contain and the details they reveal. All
nature becomes more interesting when you develop this
habit. You study a tree for its wonderful balance of large
and small parts, straight and curved lines, density and
openness. A seashell offers a lovely study in proportion
and design.

Nature is ever our inspiration—not to be copied but
to stimulate. There is beauty in the porcelain fruits
made by ancient Oriental artists; we recognize them by
line or detail but not because they are a duplication of
natural fruit. How pleasing is the work of present-day
craftsmen in Mexico who make flowers of brilliant
colored paper. Yet they are not exact copies.

I am horrified by the mass-produced artificial flowers
that are inundating our shops. In office buildings, hotel
lobbies, and homes, I see these dreadful caricatures of
nature's exquisite creations. I can only hope this fad will

pass. When fresh flowers are seen from the window, plastic ones inside are all the more disturbing. As for their use in cemeteries, they are more insult than tribute.

For those allergic to pollens, for apartment dwellers and busy housewives, there are substitutes for fresh flowers. Dried blossoms look well for a long while; straw-flowers may be grown or bought. Wayside weeds can be gathered and sprayed. Tendrils of ivy and evergreen branches make charming designs, or potted plants may be used decoratively. Handmade flowers of silk or paper or leather, bowls of fruits carved in wood, and gourds offer other possibilities for arrangements. With nature's bounty on every side, I see no excuse to degrade our taste with plastic substitutes.

It is my hope that those who read this book, and the two that have preceded it, will come to share my pleasure in collecting these wonderful natural forms. Then I hope that they will create unique and beautiful decorations with them.

ELEANOR VAN RENSSELAER

Saratoga, California
January, 1966

Contents

List of Illustrations

COLOR ILLUSTRATIONS
Between pages 10-11 and 42-43

BLACK AND WHITE

xvii

LIST OF ILLUSTRATIONS

LIST OF ILLUSTRATIONS

LIST OF ILLUSTRATIONS

1. Trees and Wreaths

Decorative little trees for tables or stands contribute pleasantly to the personality of a room. They provide a special charm of their own when fresh flowers are not available for arrangements, and are in better taste than plastic substitutes. Large trees, made to stand in tubs, can be a dominant feature in an entrance hall, or family room, or on a terrace. Whether just one kind of cone is used or many different pods and cones of varied shapes and colors, these trees, large or small, are a joy. Table trees make delightful gifts and are good sellers at fairs and bazaars. When materials are wired to a frame, the tree has a more informal, natural look, while those put together with adhesive have trim, clean lines and a formal air.

Wreaths are both Christmas decorations and year-round ornaments. Della Robbia designs, such as those shown in Illustrations 11 and 12, suggest woodcarvings and can remain on permanent display. My pupils usually make wreaths of pods and cones they have collected, which have special meaning, and include some imported pods of unusual design. These wreaths of lasting materials, when artistically designed, easily become part of your home or that of a friend. And any wreath can be dressed up a little for the holiday season with a bow or bells or a bright Christmasy background and lights.

Other Della Robbia designs are shown in my book, *Decorating with Seed Mosaics, Chipped Glass and Plant Materials,** and instructions for trees of different sizes are given in my *Decorating with Pods and Cones.***

A Note on Plant Preservatives

You can buy products from your florist which preserve natural materials. One I have found effective is Bloomlife Plastic Wax. It comes as a spray or in liquid form to be applied with a small brush. The liquid does not remove the gray patina of pods as does the spray. Greens can be kept fresh-looking for a long time and woody materials are given a clean, natural look that is not shiny because the preservative penetrates the wood.

A real advantage is that you can apply these preservatives any number of times; they do not build up a surface. Arrangements can be dusted with a soft brush or, if pieces are large, with the blower-end of a vacuum cleaner, then given a fresh application of preservative.

* Published by D. Van Nostrand (Princeton, N. J.) in 1960.
** Published by D. Van Nostrand (Princeton, N. J.) in 1957.

Adhesives

I use two kinds of adhesives in making trees and wreaths. My favorite is Plastico Rok because it dissolves in water, and cleaning hands, tools, or pods and cones is never a problem. It, however, cannot be used on outdoor decorations or over a nonporous surface or where a really sticky adhesive is needed. For these conditions I use waterproof ceramic-tile cement, available in several brands. A cleaning solvent or turpentine is needed to remove the cement. After using it I wash my hands with Boraxo detergent to remove odor and dryness. (Boraxo also removes pitch from your hands and I keep it with me on cone-collecting expeditions.) I do not use linoleum paste because, unless a large amount is applied, it dries out and materials fall from decorations.

When using an adhesive it is well to protect the work area. I lay a sheet of fiberglass—the kind frequently used for skylights or screens—on the table, since it is smooth and easy to clean and store.

Treasure Tree
(Illustration 1)

Endless variations can be made on this cone-shaped tree constructed on a hardware-cloth frame. Hardware

3

cloth is screening material of different sizes of wire mesh. It can be bought at a lumberyard or hardware store. There are a number of basic steps used in making this tree, and I will describe them in detail so you will have the techniques for devising your own treasure trees. This one is 18 inches high and has many kinds of pods and cones wired to the frame.

Make a paper pattern. Plan the height of the tree to be in scale with the pods and cones you intend to use. For this 18-inch tree I used a standard sheet of newspaper, folded. With a string 18 inches long tied around the end of a pencil (for a compass), I made a curved line from the fold to the edge of the paper by holding the end of the string at the top of the fold. Next I connected the line at the edge with the top of the fold with a ruled line. Then I cut out the fan shape and with my hand inside I opened it and rolled it into a cone. I kept rolling until it was the shape I wanted, then marked along the outside line and cut it a quarter-inch wider for overlap.

ILLUSTRATION 1

TREASURE TREE. This 18-inch tree is composed of different pods of diverse shapes, sizes, and colors, wired to a hardware-cloth frame. The tree is mounted on a black lacquer tray which rests on an inverted ceramic of cream-colored glaze with brown ridges.

4

A narrow tree form can be cut from the right angle of a paper, marking the height from edge to edge and cutting the fan shape.

Hardware-cloth Frame

Place the paper pattern flat on a piece of hardware cloth with one edge of the paper on the selvage or finished edge of the screening. Use tin snips or heavy scissors to cut out the shape. Overlap edges a quarter-inch with the selvage on the outside. Sew edges together with a fine wire—a whip stitch holds well—either using a curved needle or simply by poking the wire back and forth through the mesh. Sewing is easier if you first fasten the seam temporarily with tape. Put a strip of masking or Mystic tape around the bottom edge of the wire mesh to protect your fingers while working.

How to Install Lights

Strings of tiny lights with replaceable bulbs that slip or screw into sockets can be installed on a tree frame before you attach the pods and cones. Since sockets are usually bright green or white, I first paint them a dull gold or tan to make them as inconspicuous as possible. Mark off the places you want the lights to go with pipe cleaners or wires. The lights will be put through the

6

frame from the inside out. On a tall, narrow frame lights cannot go right to the top, but with long-nosed pliers you can get them quite high up.

Make crosscuts in the mesh frame and enlarge holes with round-nosed pliers or a dowel just big enough to hold sockets securely.

To protect the delicate bulbs take them out while putting the string in place. Let sockets hang down one or two inches outside the holes to be sure they do not slip back inside while you attach pods and cones—except at the top where a half-inch is far enough. Proceed to wire materials to the frame and when the tree is completed replace the lights in the sockets, test them and if all are in working order poke sockets back into the holes behind the pods. You can then conceal them completely with soft moss if you wish, and uncover them at Christmas time. Cord and socket can be hidden inside the tree until needed.

Attaching Wires to Scales, Pods, and Cones
(Illustration 2)

I use annealed iron wire in various sizes rather than florist wire which is coated to prevent rusting and is less flexible. For average large pods, size 22 is suitable; for smaller pods, size 24 or 26. On delicate materials I

7

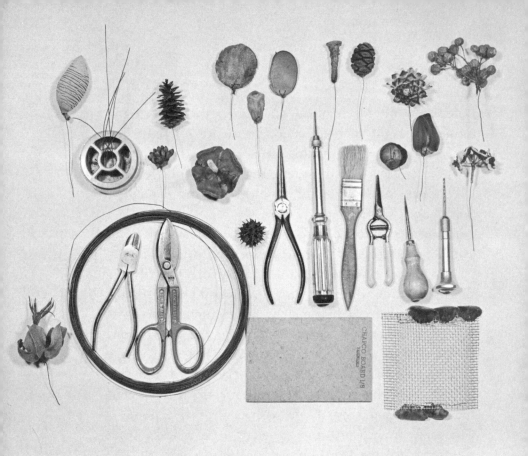

use size 28. Iron wire can be twisted very close to a pod without a tool. Hardware stores carry this kind of wire or can order it for you.

In general, one twist of wire is sufficient, unless you are using fine wire. A short end of wire goes up against the side of the pod or scale. The long end is what you attach to the hardware mesh.

SCALES AND FLAT PODS. Trim scales with small clippers

ILLUSTRATION 2

WIRING METHODS, TOOLS, AND EQUIPMENT. Wired materials, from *top left:* wire around a stem, *Zylomelum angustifolia;* western hemlock cone; three flat pods wired through two holes, jacaranda pod, cone scale, and a schotia pod; eucalyptus cap, sequoia cone and *Leucadendron plumosum;* cluster of chinaberries, stems wrapped with wire. Next row *left:* eucalyptus pod wired through one hole; deodar cone with chenille-covered wire glued in stem hole; California buckeye pod with hole drilled just below center of pod; macrozamia pod and a cluster of pittosporum pods. *Lower left:* Mexican handtree pod and a liquidambar pod to right of coil of wire.

Tools shown, from *top left:* a magnet holding cut wires; long-nosed pliers; push or Yankee drill; brush to clean pods; clippers; awl; hand drill with bit. In coil of wire are wire cutters and heavy cutters for hardware cloth. Next, a piece of hardboard to protect table when drilling. *Lower right:* a piece of $\frac{1}{8}$-inch-mesh hardware cloth with scales of fir cones wired to edges, demonstrating how wires are carried from one scale to the next, for border on tree or wreath frame; two views are shown.

9

ILLUSTRATION 5 (*top left*)
A FRAMED TREE. Large cones, berries, pods, and bits of lichen wired to hardware cloth make a dramatic tree to be seen from a distance.

ILLUSTRATION 6 (*top right*)
PRESSED LEAVES ON PLEXIGLASS PANELS. Transparent panels set into plywood sections allow enchanting interplay of sunlight and leaves.

ILLUSTRATION 7 (*bottom left*)
LACQUER TRAYS. A single transparent leaf and two butterflies embellish a round orange lacquer tray, and a colorful montage of ginkgo and liquidambar leaves enhance a square tray. Materials are glued in place and the inside of each tray is coated with resin.

ILLUSTRATION 8 (*bottom right*)
WASTEPAPER BASKET. Colorful autumn leaves, overlapped to cover the surface, are glued in place and coated with resin.

to make them as flat as possible. With a drill or awl make two holes near the base of each scale. Use 3-inch lengths of No. 24 iron wire and insert it down through one hole and back up the other, leaving one end long. Make one twist at the edge, press the short end over the edge and up against the back of the scale or flat pod to give support. (See top row in Illustration 2 for examples.)

Note: Use longer pieces of wire for materials to be attached where the cone-shaped frame gets too narrow to let you reach inside. A different method requiring more wire is used to secure materials to the uppermost section.

PODS WITH FIRM STEMS. Stems that do not snap off are easily wired. They should first be cut to about half an inch. With pod upright and stem down, hold short end of wire along the length of the stem between thumb and forefinger of left hand, pointing down. Wrap the long end around stem and short wire and back up to where pod joins stem. Press short end of wire up against the pod and bring the long end down the stem. You can make clusters of pods by wrapping wired stems together with more wire.

PODS AND COMPACT CONES (CLOSED SCALES). To attach wire to most pods, drill a small hole just above the spot where the stem was. Use an electric or hand drill, or a

12

push (Yankee) drill (shown next to brush in Illustration 2). Size of bits depends on size of pod. For really delicate pods a strong needle or awl is best.

Casuarina cones are easier to wire if you can pick them from trees when they are about to open. At this stage, when they have soft, small green stems, a wire wrapped tightly around the stem becomes embedded in it. You can open the cones if you want to by putting them in a slow oven, not more than 200 degrees F.

Deodar cones can be prepared easily with covered wire. Lay them stem-end up and where the stem came out of the cone, put a drop of glue. Then insert a length of chenille-covered wire, pipe cleaner or Twist 'N Tye wire.

Wiring Materials to a Hardware-cloth Frame

To make a border of scales, select those of similar size, put the long end of wire through the mesh, press it flat to the right against the inside of the frame. Take the second scale, place it to the right of the first with the edge just touching or slightly overlapping, and insert its wire through the mesh. Bend the first wire around the second and back against the mesh. Press the second wire flat to the right. Continue around the edge until

13

border is complete. Illustration 2 (lower right) shows how to do this.

The same procedure applies to wiring pods and cones to the frame. Work counterclockwise, from left to right, bending the wire of the adjacent piece once around the newly inserted wire, and bend the wire to the right. This method of wiring keeps materials firmly at right angles to the frame. If wires are twisted together in back of scales or pods they may droop or hang awkwardly.

When you get to the top part of the frame where it is too narrow to bend wires inside, use materials with longer wires. Then you can put the wire straight through to the opposite side of the mesh and bend the end back over the outside.

To Assemble the Tree

I put the Treasure Tree together working from the bottom up. First a border of scales of red fir. Just above, red-brown *Leucadendron plumosum* pods. Next, smooth, dark brown California buckeye pods, *Aesculus californica*. Above them are Mexican handtree pods, *Chiranthodendron pentadactylon*. Then a row of smaller leucadendron pods, lighter in color than those below. The smooth Australian pods, *Macrozamia reidlei,* of rich orange provide a dominant band of color. Above them,

14

contrasting cones of western hemlock, *Tsuga merten-siana,* which I gathered in the Sierra Nevada Mountains at 8000 feet. Fuzzy buff-colored pods of a magnolia species are topped by another row of smaller leucaden-dron, and prickly red-brown casuarina cones, *Casuarina stricta,* are next above. Finger pods, one of the forms of *Eucalyptus lehmannii* and another row of still smaller leucadendron. The textured, round gray pod above is one I have not been able to identify.

The next to top row is another species of leucaden-dron and the top, very small *Leucadendron plumosum.* Crowning the tree is a remarkable pod, probably a protea species.

Green moss and chartreuse lichen are placed between pods to add color and conceal wires. If you are using lights for your tree remember to put the globes in the sockets and push the sockets back in their holes *before* adding mosses.

I put the completed tree on a black lacquer tray and set it on an inverted ceramic.

Table Tree
(Illustration 3)

This 25-inch tree is made on a four-sided Styrofoam frame. First I camouflaged the white surface with a coat

of brown varnish—liquid shoe polish works well, too. Then I covered the whole frame, a few inches at a time, with soft green moss, pressing it into Plastico Rok adhesive, applied to the Styrofoam. Styrofoam glue could be used instead of Plastico Rok.

Next I sorted the deodar cones into four groups of graded sizes, making each group of eleven cones as well matched as possible. Because I wanted a more casual appearance than adhesive provides, I prepared the cones with 2-inch lengths of chenille-covered wires according to the procedure described above in "Attaching Wires to Scales, Pods, and Cones." I pushed the covered wires through the moss into the Styrofoam, placing cones of the same size in the same position on each of the four sides.

Very small deodar cones are not attractive, so I finished the top and spaces between cones with clustered eucalyptus pods, inserting stems directly into the frame. Their lovely green color and contrasting texture help display the handsome design of the cones.

ILLUSTRATION 3

TABLE TREE. Brown deodar cones in straight rows are combined with deep green eucalyptus pods and bits of moss in this table tree on a four-sided Styrofoam frame.

With the dimensions of the tree now apparent, I could select an appropriate trunk. It is often easier to choose a properly proportioned trunk after the basic tree is made. For this one I used a section of Christmas tree, stored from the previous season, with nice branching. I trimmed the branches and left about 4 inches of trunk above them which I inserted into a hole in the exact center of the Styrofoam. The branches gave firm support to the tree, and contributed interesting detail.

A fluted copper bowl related well to both the form and color of the deodar cones. I set the trunk in small rocks in plaster of Paris (see directions below) and after covering the surface with glue, sprinkled brown seeds over the top.

To Secure Tree Trunks in Containers

The trunk of a small tree can be held in a cup with a dab of Plastico Rok adhesive and a little paraffin or candle wax. Wax alone will not support a tree since it melts if placed in a warm spot.

For large trees I use plaster of Paris. My method is this: I pour the amount of water I think is right into a paper cup and slowly add plaster, a spoonful at a time until it comes to a peak above the water. I let this set until plaster is absorbed into the water, then stir *slowly* to prevent air bubbles from forming. When it is the consistency of whipped cream I pour the plaster through a funnel into the container around the trunk to an inch or two from the rim. Plaster can be covered with seeds or pebbles sprinkled over a surface of glue or held in place with a lacquer spray, even hair spray.

A Tapered Tree on a Rattan Frame
(Illustration 5)

Deodar and casuarina cones, combined with orange safflowers, are wired to this slender, 40-inch-high rattan frame. Instead of using the stand shown in Illustration 4, I selected a sturdy branch to be the trunk and set it in plaster of Paris in a bonsai planter, using stones to conceal the plaster. Before attaching the cones I reinforced the lower part of the frame with heavy wire where the spaces between the rattan strips were too wide.

Each cone had a single wire attached to it, and I wound each wire to the rattan or wire strip. I began working at the top, making alternating rows of small deodar and casuarina cones, sticking the wire straight through to the opposite side, and fastening it as far down the tree as possible. Working downward I used successively larger cones; the lowest area is all deodar cones—not by plan, but because I used up all my large

19

ILLUSTRATION 4

RATTAN TREE FRAME. A 40-inch rattan frame with detachable stand is the structure for the Tapered Tree, Illustration 5. On the left are wired cones and safflowers ready to be attached to the frame. On the right are a coil of No. 18 wire to fill spaces between rattan strips, pliers to cut wire, and long-nosed pliers to reach into frame and adjust wires.

casuarina cones (*Casuarina stricta*) in the process of constructing the tree. After the cones were attached, I filled in all the little spaces with wired orange safflowers. When I finished the tree I sprayed it with a plant preservative (see preceding "Note on Plant Preservatives") and perched a golden squirrel on top.

Eucalyptus Tree
(Illustration 6)

Using one species of rust-brown eucalyptus pods throughout the tree and another for the top, Mary Elizabeth Schwarz has constructed a lively 16-inch tree on a Styrofoam form. Tucked between the brown pods are bits of bright green sphagnum moss. The tree rests on a cardboard circle bordered with individual scales of mountain pine (*Pinus monticola*). An inverted ceramic cup supports the tree; its rich glossy brown glaze is an attractive contrast to the dull-surfaced pods.

Mrs. Schwarz used a gray ceramic-tile cement through-

ILLUSTRATION 5

TAPERED TREE. Alternating rows of deodar and casuarina cones with orange safflowers filling spaces throughout, form this 40-inch tree on a rattan frame. Trunk is a branch anchored in plaster of Paris in a bonsai planter.

out. She colored this with Universal burnt-sienna tinting color to match the pods and to make it easier to conceal the adhesive.

Small Trees
(Illustration 7)

Mrs. Schwarz again demonstrates her interest in designing with one kind of material. These charming little trees are made with tiny half-inch cones, *Casuarina cunninghamiana,* attached with ceramic-tile cement to Styrofoam forms. In proper scale are the golden china-berry spirals and tops of beechnut cones with china-berry centers. The largest tree has a eucalyptus pod at the top. Cardboard circles with crisp borders of mountainpine scales support the trees which are placed on inverted Japanese saki cups. The largest tree is on a tea cup. These trees make unusual table decorations and interesting gifts.

If chinaberries are unfamiliar to you, you may know

ILLUSTRATION 6
EUCALYPTUS TREE. This gay little tree made by Mary Elizabeth Schwarz suggests the variations possible with just one kind of material, the pod of a species of eucalyptus that looks like tiny bells.

ILLUSTRATION 7

FOUR SMALL TREES. Tiny cones of *Casuarina cunninghamiana*
here make compact little trees, decorated with spirals of round
yellow chinaberries and topknots of beechnut cones with china-
berry centers. A eucalyptus pod crowns the tallest tree. Japanese
saki cups and a tea cup serve as bases. These trees were made
by Mary Elizabeth Schwarz.

them as pods from the umbrella tree (*Melia azedarach*). In Texas and Oklahoma these trees produce pods which look almost like porcelain. Those from the interior valley in California do not have such a delicate appearance.

A Victorian Tree with Lights
(Illustrations 8, 9 and Color Illustration 1)

This tree is made on a parasol frame covered with quarter-inch-mesh hardware cloth. (Florists can usually order this kind of frame for you from a wireworks or wire wholesaler.) I made a paper pattern for half the frame as a guide for the amount of hardware cloth needed to cover the frame completely. The pattern is shown in Illustration 8. Then I cut out the two halves of the mesh, trimmed the edges with tin snips and, using a curved needle threaded with soft wire, whipped the mesh sections together. I attached them to the frame by whipping soft wire over alternate ribs. I then trimmed around the edge to match the mesh to the curves of the frame, and whipped the edge with wire.

When the hardware cloth was in place, I selected spots for lights. This string has thirty-five amber lights and after the sockets were decorated with dull gold paint, I marked holes for them along the ribs and in a cluster

27

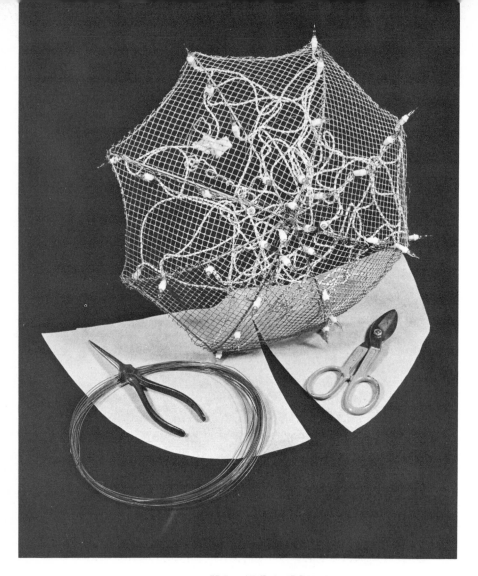

ILLUSTRATION 8

USING A PARASOL FRAME. This frame, covered with mesh hardware cloth, is the structure for the Victorian tree (Color Illustration 1). Shown also are the paper pattern, No. 24 wire, tin snips,
and long-nosed pliers. A string of small lights is attached to the
mesh along the ribs of the frame and at the top.

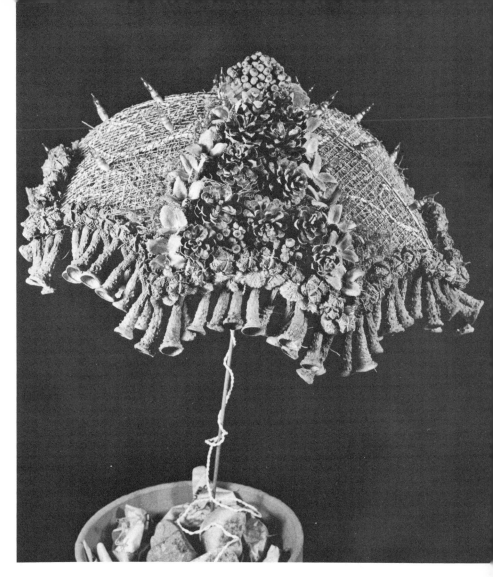

ILLUSTRATION 9

CONSTRUCTION OF VICTORIAN TREE. This shows the lichen padding on the underside, the fringe of long narrow eucalyptus caps
and the edging of bright red cockscomb with deep red eucalyptus
caps. One section has been completed. I put the handle of the
parasol in a wooden planter with rocks to support it while
working. (Color Illustration 1 shows the finished tree.)

at the top. I cut holes in the mesh, then enlarged them slightly with long-nosed pliers. Working from the top down, I inserted the sockets from underneath to the outside, making sure the plug end came down along the handle, and wrapped the handle with wire.

To conceal the electric cord and to help hold it in place, I padded the underside with true Spanish moss, gathered near New Orleans. Gray lichen, found on live oaks in California (also called Spanish moss) could be used instead. A lining of felt could be made by drawing a paper pattern for it before adding material to the frame. I wired the moss on with fine wire threaded through a large-eyed needle, placing a long piece over the length of the moss and attaching it to the outside of the mesh. Use just enough wire to hold the moss, since wires from pods and cones will make it secure.

Pods and cones came next. I started with the dangles —red, green, and tan caps from one of the eucalyptus pods, *Eucalyptus megacornuta.* Other possibilities are carob or wisteria pods or any curled beanlike pods. I drilled a hole in the tip of each pod (hand or electric drill) and put a 2-inch piece of No. 24 iron wire through, making a loop close to the pod (no need to twist). See Illustration 2 and "Attaching Wires." The other end of wire I put over the rim of the frame,

30

wrapped it around once and stuck the remaining piece up into the wire mesh.

After the dangles I put on a row of deep red caps of *Eucalyptus erythrocorys.* Ends were first trimmed with clippers to make them as flat as possible and a hole drilled in the base of the pod for a wire. To keep these pods straight up, I press the wire through the mesh and lichen, then bend it against the frame directly under the pod and hook it up through the mesh.

Next I worked on the top section. I wired on a circle of eight brown, flocked-looking,. egg-shaped pods that I have not been able to identify, and in the center of the lights, wired on a cluster of dried, orange pyracantha berries. Since the stems are short I poured transparent glue over the berries to be sure they stayed in place.

Note: One method for drying pyracantha berries is to put berry-laden branches in water for several weeks, then clip off clusters and store them in an open box in the dark for several weeks more. The dried berries are smaller than before but a fine deep orange.

I selected open beechnut cones that are a light brown on the inside to go along the ribs of the frame next to the lights. First I graded them into sizes to have larger cones at the bottom and smaller cones at the top. I drilled a hole in the back of each cone, put a 3-inch

31

piece of No. 24 iron wire through the hole, and pressed the short end against the cone (again just a loop, not a twist). The long end is stuck through the mesh, pressed at a right angle to the cone off to one side, and hooked back through the mesh.

Red-brown lodge-pole pine cones fill the sections. I graded them according to size, cutting away the backs of some with garden snips to get the size I needed, and counted out the approximate number for each section. These cones are wired by putting wire around open scales near the stem end, halfway around the cone, and pulling both ends of the wire together, twisting once and pressing the short end up against the side of the cone. (See Illustration 2.) This provides good support. To keep things in proportion, I put larger cones in the lower portion and small ones at the top.

Sprays of pyracantha berries and bits of soft green moss were used throughout to cover up any exposed wire.

To complete this part of the tree I glued tufts of red cockscomb under the caps at the edge above the dangles, then painted on preservative—liquid Bloomlife Plastic Wax—with a small brush. (To use a spray such as Flora-Set or Floral Spray, you first have to cover up the lights.)

To make the trunk I wired on a stout thistle stalk to

32

the parasol handle and wrapped the light cord around it. Then, with heavy pliers, I shortened the handle by twisting the end into a flat circle that would fit into the bottom of the container. Fine copper wire holds carefully spaced, greenish-brown stems of Ahanui pods from Hawaii along the length of the trunk. Raffia of the same green-brown is glued over the wire.

A tub of light wood, given a maple stain, serves as container. It has little sections of wood on the bottom that raise the tub up, so I could drill a hole for the cord in the bottom. If you use a tub that isn't raised, drill a hole in the side. You may have to remove the plug if the hole is small, and if you do I advise making a diagram of just where each wire comes from as you take the plug apart—especially if it is from Italy!

Little rocks held the trunk while I added plaster of Paris (see preceding "To Secure Tree Trunks in Containers"). I spread a layer of glue on top, sprinkled flaky red-brown seeds over it, and pressed them in place.

Strawflower Tree

(Color Illustration 9)

This 18-inch tree is made with wired strawflowers of sunny yellow, orange, and bronze hues. Stems are replaced with wires that are held together to form the

33

trunk of the tree. (If you grow your own strawflowers, pick them just before they open. Trim the stem off close to the flower and insert an 8- or 9-inch piece of florist wire into the back while flowers are still fresh. When they dry, the wire is securely in place.)

I began with yellow blossoms at the top and progressed, a row at a time, to orange and bronze. As I placed each flower between the thumb and forefinger of my left hand, I made a bend in the wire. At the top, the angle is very slight, but increases as the tree grows. Each flower looks directly out of the tree and the shape of the tree is determined by the length of the right angle turn of the wire. After each row I wound a separate light wire around the wires keeping them parallel and neat. About half way down the tree I began shortening the turn of the wire, decreasing the size of the tree. The bottom row of flowers turns slightly downward to hide the construction. A twist of the extra wire around the wires of the trunk holds the tree in shape. Then I wrapped the trunk with florist tape.

Trees may be constructed in any shape by this method. With cones instead of flowers attached to wires, similar trees can be made.

I selected a heavy brass cup for the container. Then I decided on the length of the trunk. Where the wires

34

would rest on the bottom of the cup, I again wrapped them tightly with soft wire, took pliers and turned the ends up all the way around to fit against the sides of the cup and help support the tree. If necessary, cut off wires an inch or two below the rim of the container.

Before adding plaster, I put a small wad of modeling clay in the bottom to hold the trunk while pouring. Then I mixed the plaster (see preceding "To Secure Tree Trunks in Containers") and used a funnel to guide it into the cup.

To achieve a formal effect I wrapped a piece of half-inch gold velvet ribbon over the floral-taped trunk down to the plaster surface, using glue to hold the ribbon in place. The plaster is concealed by pale yellow seeds attached with glue and coated with Floral Spray. Another way to decorate this kind of trunk is to apply Plastico Rok adhesive to the wrapped wires and press seeds onto it. This gives the effect of bark.

Della Robbia Wreaths

A Della Robbia wreath is one made of a variety of pods, cones, leaves, and dried flowers. Materials are distributed to show each piece to advantage. Contrasts in texture, color, shape, and size help to achieve this while a sense of natural growth is retained. Wires attached to

35

the materials should keep the feeling of stems, and awkward or artificial placement is to be avoided.

The two wreaths which follow (Illustrations 11 and 12) are constructed on double wire frames (Illustration 10). Small frames can be made of wire coat hangers, and larger frames of heavy steel wire are available at hardware stores. All sizes can be bought already made (see "Sources of Supplies")—a great convenience when preparing a number of wreaths for a bazaar.

Before adding materials to the frame, select a backing. Make a pattern by laying the frame on it and drawing the outlines of both inner and outer rims. Heavy card-

---

ILLUSTRATION 10

WREATH CONSTRUCTION. A double wire frame, wrapped with crisscrossed wire to hold moss padding, is shown with one section completed between two deodar cones. The wood rack, available at The Fir Tree (see Sources of Supplies), holds the frame in a good working position. A chenille marker at the top indicates place for the third deodar cone. Duplicate sets of pods and cones will be used to complete the other two sections. An araucaria scale at the top of the wreath shows method of putting on a border.

At left hangs a cardboard backing. Holes will be made with an awl or leather punch about a quarter-inch in from each edge. Fine wire passed through holes and laced to wire hoops of the completed wreath will attach backing.

board or sheet cork can be used for frames up to 14 inches in diameter. For larger backings use masonite or plywood. Make a number of holes around both edges about 4 inches apart on cardboard and at longer intervals on rigid backings. Then, after completing the wreath, attach the backing with light wire put through holes and whipped over the edges.

Both Della Robbia wreaths illustrated are made in three matched sections, with a general distribution to let the eye move easily around the wreath. It is important not to lose the rhythm by overemphasis on any one part.

To give body to a wreath I wrap the frame with wire in a crisscross fashion, making a mesh base for a padding of moss or lichen. Green-gray California Spanish moss is wiry and meshlike when dried. Gray Spanish moss from the south also makes a good pad as does chartreuse staghorn lichen which grows on the north side of trees in the Sierra Nevada Mountains of California. This lichen provides a colorful background for the brown pods and cones. One of my students used horsehair bought from an upholsterer; lightweight wire wrapped around the padding and frame held it in place.

In selecting my material for a Della Robbia wreath I lay out three of each kind of pod and cone as nearly matched in size and color as possible. With pipe cleaners or pencils I mark three equidistant places on the moss padding, then replace them with the pod or cone that is to be the center of interest in that section.

All materials are prepared with a single wire (see preceding "Attaching Wires"). Each wire is pushed through the moss to the back where I twist three or four ends together *lightly,* allowing changes to be made while working on the wreath. The single wire makes it easy to adjust the angle of the pod or cone.

When all materials are satisfactorily placed, lay the wreath face down on a pad of crumpled paper or any soft material. Now twist wires firmly together, trim with wire cutters leaving about an inch of twisted wires. Use tapered pliers to turn this twist deep into the moss to make the back flat. Then attach backing to the frame with light wire using a whip stitch through holes and over both rims.

When a wreath is completed I turn it to different positions to decide which section should be at the top. Then I wire a heavy brass or plastic ring to the backing and outer wire on the frame. Wire through two holes secures the ring more firmly than through one.

Large Wreath
(Illustration 11)

A 30-inch double wire frame is the basis for this Della Robbia wreath. After wrapping the frame with wire to make a base for the moss, I attached *Araucaria bidwillii* scales to the inside rim. Illustration 10 shows how this is done. The wired end of the scale overlaps the inner hoop of the frame. Scales can be placed to overlap or just touch, with wire brought across the frame, turned over the outside edge and pressed back. After scales are attached, add the moss and mark off three equal sections before adding pods and completing the wreath. Full directions are given above in "Della Robbia Wreaths."

Beginning with the large lotus pod at the top and reading counterclockwise, materials are as follows: a ruddy pomegranate, open Aleppo pine cone and pod of ginger above, an immature sugar pine cone, cluster of orange safflowers, spider eucalyptus pod, bird of paradise pod, small, open, yellow pine cone, a deodar cone,

---

ILLUSTRATION 11
LARGE WREATH. Araucaria scales form the inner border on this Della Robbia wreath of varied pods, cones, and dried flowers placed in three matching sections on a 30-inch frame.

ILLUSTRATION 9 (*top left*)
STRAWFLOWER TREE. Large wired strawflowers in gold, orange, and bronze hues make this colorful, compact 18-inch tree.

ILLUSTRATION 10 (*top right*)
CENTERPIECE OR WALL ORNAMENT. Fuchsia-shaped resin leaves are wired together with glass tubes for fresh flowers, such as these dainty white campanulas.

ILLUSTRATION 11 (*bottom left*)
CANDLE CENTERPIECE. Colorful dried flowers and sphagnum moss are glued to an 8-inch circle of masonite to make this pretty base for a large candle. The lei is gold ribbon decorated with moss and acacia, attached to the candle with tapelike clay.

ILLUSTRATION 12 (*bottom right*)
PLEXIGLASS PANEL. Petals of resin molded on *Osmanthus ilicifolia* leaves are composed into flowers with eucalyptus caps for centers. Red plexiglass is glued to a backing of yellow felt on cardboard.

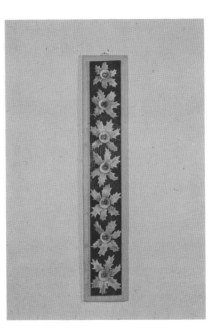

ILLUSTRATION 13 *(top left)*

BUTTERFLY. A variety of seeds is glued to a transparent background of mylar and covered with plastic resin to make this rattan frame a gay, colorful wall ornament.

ILLUSTRATION 14 *(top right)*

RATTAN LEAF MOSAICS. Colorful seeds in rattan frames are backed with mylar and coated with resin.

ILLUSTRATION 15 *(bottom left)*

SEA-GLASS PICTURE. On a 6- by 9-inch piece of blue plexiglass, mounted on a sheet of spun aluminum, a little scene is made of colorful bits of glass, smoothed and frosted by sand and sea.

SEA GLASS IN A RATTAN STAR. Lavender, blue, and blue-green pieces of glass, combined with milky white chips, are fitted to a piece of mylar in a gilded rattan frame.

ILLUSTRATION 16 *(bottom right)*

MAGNOLIA PETALS AND LEAVES. These resin castings are glued to orange plexiglass and set in a frame of brown cork.

large cluster of pods of agave (century plant), another open yellow pine cone, an araucaria seed removed from one of the scales, prickly liquidambar pod, and a coconut calyx.

Next is an earpod with a cluster of wooden cherries and an oriental poppy pod with a fuzzy-textured, mustard-colored bottle tree pod and mountain pine cone. A Joshua tree pod, the spiked base of a deodar cone, a cedrela pod, a cluster of hakea pods, and a golden yarrow flower follow.

Next come a curled bean-shaped pod, an open jacaranda pod, a eucalyptus pod in flower, the same pod with caps still on, and a magnolia pod above. Below are a sequoia and a casuarina cone. A hickory fruit, jimson weed pod, the orange base of the leaf of a dragon tree, devil's claw, bishop pine cone, the open side of a piñon cone, a cluster of lipstick pods, golden cockscomb, and a stem of screw beans.

Della Robbia Wreath
(Illustration 12)

Constructed on a 20-inch double wire frame, this wreath of pods from Australia, South Africa, Hawaii, and California measured 24 inches in diameter when completed. A border of bunya-bunya scales from large cones

ILLUSTRATION 12

DELLA ROBBIA WREATH. Pods from Australia, South Africa, Hawaii, and California are combined in three sections on a double wire frame, 20 inches in diameter.

45

is attached to the outer rim. The three matching sections are delineated with three large sculptural *Banksia larisina* pods.

Materials used in each section are (reading counterclockwise from the top banksia pod and Douglas fir cone just below it): a cluster of chinaberries and a sequoia cone; to the side, a *Leucadendron plumosum* and spray of white statice; above, a small Aleppo pine cone, screw beans, and an orange *Macrozamia reidlei*. At top, two bottle tree pods, a prickly round lipstick pod, a California hemlock cone, a partly opened jacaranda pod, an open oleander pod, and a gray, fish-shaped *Zylomelum angustifolia*.

Next, a clustered form of eucalyptus, a jimson weed pod, two bell-shaped eucalyptus pods, an earpod, two hakea pods, two other forms of eucalyptus, a wide open California hemlock cone, a large *Eucalyptus macrocarpa*, a deodar cone, another macrozamia, a California buckeye pod, and one section of a pod from a trumpet vine resembling a milkweed pod.

The large seed from a scale of bunya-bunya cone follows; then a small *Leucadendron plumosum,* an inverted tubular cap and pod of eucalyptus, an open Aleppo pine cone (creamy inside because I opened it in the oven when it was still green), a large casuarina cone, a coconut calyx, a leucadendron species that looks like a pine cone, a small dark yellow bottle tree pod, a beautifully modeled, shiny brown tropical palm, more white statice, a cotton pod, a piñon cone, a Mexican hand-tree calyx, two hakea pods, and a ridged *Leucadendron sabulosum* nestled against the banksia pod.

Wreath of Magnolia Leaves
(Illustration 13)

Glossy gold and brown magnolia leaves can be made into impressive wreaths to decorate a room or doorway any time of the year. The leaves should be treated first to make them easy to handle and to preserve their color.

PREPARE THE LEAVES. For the wreath illustrated, I used leaves treated with Propylene Glycol, a product that makes the leaves a richer, more attractive color and one that is less expensive than glycerin. (See "Sources of Supplies.") I make a solution of about equal parts of Propylene Glycol and hot water and place large branches of magnolia with stems cut on a slant in the solution, adding more water as the mixture is absorbed. (This process is most effective during the months when sap is moving in the branches.)

SORT LEAVES ACCORDING TO SIZE. You will need a good many leaves to make a 28-inch wreath like the one

47

illustrated. Sort them into sizes: small leaves for the inside edge, medium for the outside edge, and two large ones to go between. A smaller or narrower wreath would need only one large leaf in the center of a row.

CONSTRUCT THE FRAME. This wreath is made on a 28-inch frame of heavy cardboard 5 inches wide. The size of a wreath will depend on the shape and size of the leaves. Keep in mind that the leaves overlap both edges of the frame by several inches, and the completed wreath is therefore larger than the frame.

Draw the wreath outline on heavy cardboard, then cut the outside edge with scissors, the inside with a razor-blade cutter. Lay the cardboard frame on a piece of thin plywood, masonite, or corrugated box material, and trace the outline. Cut out the backing, make matching holes in each frame 8 to 10 inches apart just inside each rim. Set the backing aside until the leaves are in place on the cardboard.

ASSEMBLE THE WREATH. Cut stems off the leaves. With

ILLUSTRATION 13

WREATH OF MAGNOLIA LEAVES. Warm brown leaves, treated with Propylene Glycol, are stapled to a 28-inch cardboard frame with masonite backing. A Jeffrey cone and a group of larger magnolia leaves ornament the wreath.

49

a heavy stapler, staple each leaf across the center rib near the stem end to the cardboard in rows. Use a small leaf on the inside, pointing in, a medium leaf on the outside edge, pointing out, and two large leaves in the middle overlapping to fill the space. (Illustration 14 shows the technique.)

Work in one direction all around the wreath, making sure each succeeding row covers the staples on the leaves behind. If it is awkward to staple a particular leaf in place, use a dab of Plastico Rok or ceramic-tile adhesive to hold it.

To ornament the completed wreath, staple a grouping of extra large leaves at an angle to the outer rim and attach a cone or cluster of pods with wires at their base.

ATTACH THE BACKING. First hold the completed wreath up to decide how you want to hang it, with any decoration or heavier section in the appropriate position. Wire a small curtain ring to the backing through one of the holes near the edge at the top. Then match the holes on the border of the cardboard to those on the backing. Put light, flexible wire through the holes to tie the two frames together.

Crescent of Magnolia Leaves
(Illustration 14)

Overlapping magnolia leaves may be made into an attractive crescent with or without additional decorative material. I have combined a large brown lotus pod, sprays of reddish volcano grass, and a cluster of wooden cherries to embellish the leaves. Some leaves were picked green and dried in the dark to retain their soft green color; others were left on branches treated with Propylene Glycol solution (see preceding "Wreath of Magnolia Leaves") and picked when I was ready to use them. They are golden or dark brown.

This crescent frame is made from a 22-inch square of quarter-inch mesh, but could also be made on cardboard. First make a paper pattern. Fold paper so the sides will be identical and draw the outline. It can be wide or narrow, with long or short arms. I frequently cut out several patterns and select the one with the best proportions. Use the same pattern for both the hardware cloth and a backing material of thin masonite or pegboard. (Instructions for assembling are also given in the preceding "Wreath of Magnolia Leaves.")

Remove stems from the magnolia leaves and sort into matching pairs of graded sizes. Plan to work from the

tips of the crescent down toward the center, gradually increasing the size of the leaves, starting with small ones at the tips. Match the angle of placement on each arm of the crescent.

To attach leaves to the hardware cloth, insert both ends of short lengths of lightweight No. 24 wire into each leaf on either side of the center rib near the stem end. Put the wire through the mesh, and twist the two ends together with *one* twist on the back of the frame. Press wires very flat and trim off the ends. When all the leaves are in place, wire on any decorative material you wish. Then attach the backing to the wire frame following the directions for the preceding wreath.

Apply a clear plant preservative when crescent is completed.

ILLUSTRATION 14

CONSTRUCTION OF A CRESCENT OF MAGNOLIA LEAVES ON HARD-WARE CLOTH. Leaves, tools, preservative, pegboard backing, a piece of the hardware cloth frame, and the assembled sections of leaves with a lotus pod, volcano grass, and a cluster of wooden cherries are shown here to explain the various steps in making a crescent of leaves.

2. For a Merry Christmas

Nature's offerings collected from gardens, fields, and the roadside can be designed into decorations for the Christmas holidays. Branches of evergreen, wreaths and stars of pods and cones with lights, bells, and bright trees are part of Christmas pleasure. In this chapter I describe projects that various members of the family can enjoy making—place mats from Christmas cards for the younger ones, and a star of cones glowing with lights for those more skilled. Baskets piled with shapely cones, embellished perhaps with handcrafted birds and decked out with gay ribbons make warm-hearted gifts. May your Christmas and that of your friends be the merrier for the suggestions you find here and throughout this book.

A Christmas Welcome with Lights
(Illustration 15)

A handsome board of Douglas fir (*Pseudotsuga taxifolia*) with natural tones of lavender and gold, is the background for a Christmas greeting. This piece of 1-inch by 12-inch shelving is 38 inches long and coated

ILLUSTRATION 15

A CHRISTMAS WELCOME. Bright red Brazilian pepper berries spell out the Christmas greeting on a board of knotty wood, decorated with Port Orford cedar and tiny lights.

ILLUSTRATION 16

PINE-CONE BELLS. Jeffrey pine cone trimmed with lodge-pole cones have clappers of liquidambar balls or large casuarina cones to ring in the Christmas season. Gold satin ribbon adds a festive touch to this decoration hung from a cedar plaque.

with Deft Wood Finish to give the wood a soft natural polish. On the back I nailed a raised notch bar hanger (available in art supply stores) before proceeding to decorate.

The letters were first drawn freehand in 2¼-inch squares on paper, then traced with carbon paper on the board. I selected red Brazilian pepper berries (*Schinus terebinthifolius*) for the letters, but other red seeds like dry nadina or pyracantha berries, false wiliwili (*Adenanthera pavonina*), or those orange-red berries with a black dot (*Abrus precatorius*, confusingly termed black-eyed Susan) would be equally Christmasy.

Working on a small area at a time, I applied a little glue, and with fingers and tweezers, I pressed the berries close together within the letter outlines. To keep them firm, I brushed on a resin product, Natcol Poly Coat. A Jeffrey pine cone, sawed in half, is attached at the top and bottom with ceramic-tile cement.

I stapled a string of 24 lights (the small ones in varied colors) all around the edge of the board, using staples wide enough to go over the base of the sockets and hold them securely against the sides. Extra cord between lights is tacked to the back. Then I completed the decoration with branches of Port Orford cedar (*Chamaecyparis lawsoniana*) with little cones. Any evergreen that

56

does not shed its needles when dry can be used—juniper, redwood, pine, or incense cedar. To attach greens to the board I used a small staple, first putting the staple over the stem, then pressing the staple on the board with my thumb and tacking it down firmly with a tack hammer. Cord between lights is hidden by the pieces of greens. After Christmas you can remove the evergreens easily and store the board for the next season.

Pine-cone Bells
(Illustration 16)

For a sizable front-door decoration, the large Jeffrey pine cones (*Pinus jeffreyi*) make attractive bells. These can be given a bell shape by attaching lodge-pole cones (*Pinus murrayana*) around the bottom. There are two ways of doing this: if the Jeffrey cone has wide open scales I push the smaller cone—with a dab of brown Plastico Rok or ceramic-tile cement on its base—between the scales; otherwise I pull out a row of scales with pliers and attach the small cones with adhesive. (Plastico Rok is water soluble and can be washed off if it smears. You can use glue, but it takes a large amount to hold the cones in place.)

When the bells are made I turn them upside down in a coffee can to trim off the stem end and make the bell

57

flat. Then I drill a hole in the center of the stem section. The clappers in this decoration are liquidambar balls and large casuarina cones, each prepared with a loop of fine wire. I measure lengths of fine wire wrapped in raffia a little longer than the length I need for the clapper, put one end through the loop in the clapper and twist it to hold it neatly. I wrap the other end of the wired raffia with fine wire, apply glue, and slip it into the hole in the cone bell.

I make the bows by pulling crossed-over loops of ribbon together in the middle with fine wire that I then fasten to the top of the bell. After this I wire on a piece of narrow ribbon to the top of each bell. To assemble, I pin the long ribbons together in the sequence I want, then glue them.

For the top I prepared a cedar plaque, first nailing a firm hanger on the back, then gluing the ribbons in place, and securing them with thumbtacks. The border is made of lodge-pole cone "daisies." These were slightly damaged cones, with good color, put to new use by pulling out the center scales with pliers to make them look like flowers. I fastened them on with Plastico Rok.

Further decorative touches on the plaque might include lettering or mounted Christmas cards (glued on,

58

then coated with lacquer to blend them with the wood). You might also want to spray the cones with flat white or red paint, or gild them perhaps, after making them into bells.

Fan of Large Cones
(Illustration 17)

This fan-shaped decoration, 25 inches high and 28 inches across is an interesting way to display a fine collection of cones. It can be used in the fireplace or on the mantle or, if embellished with a ribbon or bells, become a more seasonal decoration. I selected mountain pine cones (*Pinus monticola*) for the main part of the fan, a sliced Jeffrey pine cone (*Pinus jeffreyi*) for the center, the scales curled by placing it in a slow oven. Five immature sugar pine cones (*Pinus lambertiana*) and two curved knob-cone pine cones (*Pinus attenuata*) radiate from the center.

To make this decoration, first cut a paper pattern to size (with your supply of cones in mind). This pattern should be wider down near the base than you want the finished decoration to be because, after completing the decoration, you need to bend the sides back somewhat to make the fan curve out. With the pattern as guide,

59

ILLUSTRATION 17

A FAN OF LARGE CONES. Mountain pine, sugar and knob-cone
pine cones, and a section of Jeffrey pine, are mounted on
hardware cloth and backed with board to make a handsome
fireplace or mantle decoration.

cut the fan shape from quarter-inch-mesh hardware cloth. Bind the edges with brown masking tape to protect your fingers. Save the pattern to use later.

Remove stems from the cones. Work with No. 22 wire cut into 7-inch lengths. Put one end of the wire halfway around each cone through the scales at the base. *Press it flat against the base of the cone.* This provides additional support and keeps the wire out of the way when attaching the cone to the mesh frame. It also lets you control the angle at which you place the cone.

To attach a cone, put the remaining end of the wire through the mesh and press it at a right angle against the mesh and back through again, then bend wire over. This keeps the back flat and allows you to replace or adjust a cone. If you twist wires together, it is difficult to make changes and may interfere with the backing material that goes on later.

Start at the lower center with the section of Jeffrey pine. (To anchor this piece I put *both* ends of the wire through the mesh.) Then place the five sugar pine cones, pointing them up to create a sense of depth. These go slightly under the Jeffrey cone which is pulled tightly against the ends of the sugar pines. Put the knob-cone cones below the center with ends pointed down.

Sort the mountain pine cones into large and small.

61

Place the large ones throughout the fan and the small ones around the edge. Point them up away from the mesh frame. Tuck chartreuse staghorn lichen around the center cone and around the rim of the fan.

To make the fan bow out, attach three wires across the back at the side edges and tighten them until you have the curve you want. Then lay the fan on the original paper pattern and trace around it to get the new outline. Draw this on the backing material (I used hardboard) and saw it out. Drill several holes around the edge and fasten the backing to the mesh frame with wire. To keep the center from sagging I put a block of wood between the hardware cloth and backing, attaching it with ceramic-tile cement to the hardboard before wiring the backing in place. Bits of staghorn lichen around the edges cover any gaps or wires.

Attach a strong hanger. Since this is a heavy arrangement, two screws with wire between is advisable.

Christmas Card Decorations
(Illustration 18)

Christmas cards are a continuing source of colorful reproductions of paintings or original designs which you can cut out and apply to various ornamented backings. A reproduction of Raphael's lovely "Alba Madonna" fits well into the center of this flat wooden plate. I used white glue for the picture and transparent glue for an edging of wired gold braid. A circle of rosy California pepper berries is held with glue also, then coated with Natcol Poly Coat resin. At the edge of the plate on the back I glued a piece of wide gold rickrack, allowing half of it to be seen from the front. This plate has a small hanger on the back.

The friendship motto is mounted on a piece of cardboard which has a fabric hanger glued to the back. For a neat edging I glued on wired gold cord and decorated the card design with two kinds of flowers—little pink and white acrocliniums I had dried myself and tiny creamy-white strawflowers from the florist. The flowers are glued in place and painted with resin, Natcol Poly Coat, which makes them look like porcelain.

Note: To dry acrocliniums, pick them when they open wide in the bright sun. Put their stems through a piece of hardware cloth laid on top of an open carton. In a few days the flowers are crisp and dry and still colorful. Do plant them in your summer garden.

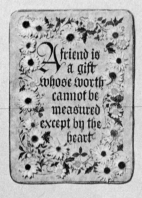

A friend is
a gift
whose worth
cannot be
measured
except by the
heart

Placemats of Christmas Cards
(Illustrations 19 and 20)

A gay family project and one well suited to Christmas bazaars is turning cards of previous years into decorative placemats. In addition to a large assortment of Christmas cards you will need a bottle of white glue and medium-weight posterboard (white or colored) cut into mats 11 by 17 inches. My art supply store lets me use their cutting board for this purpose, and I can get three mats from one sheet of posterboard. Otherwise, a metal right-angle square is helpful and scissors with heavy blades. The other ingredient is a roll of transparent 18-inch-wide Con-tact, a product similar to the shelving material with the same brand name, and found in hardware or department stores. For borders, pressed leaves, grasses, or evergreen tips give a nice touch, but anything can be

---

ILLUSTRATION 18

DECORATED CHRISTMAS CARDS. Lovely reproductions of paintings or original designs from cards can be made into wall decorations. At top, a reproduction of a painting is glued to a wooden tray and decorated with California pepper berries, gold braid, and rickrack. Below, a motto mounted on cardboard is embellished with resin-treated pink and white acrocliniums.

65

ILLUSTRATION 19

CHRISTMAS CARD PLACEMATS. Bright cards, full of Christmas spirit, are glued to posterboard and covered with transparent Con-tact. Leaves make interesting borders.

ILLUSTRATION 20

used from gold paper to cutouts of colored papers made with pinking shears.

Sort the cards into compatible groups as to theme, style, color, and size. Select some for each mat, trim off parts you don't want, and arrange on the posterboard. Then make the border. After all parts are satisfactory, apply white glue to each piece and press carefully in place.

For each mat cut a 12-inch strip of the Con-tact using the marked line on the paper backing as a guide. Peel off the paper and lay the transparent sheet on the table, sticky side up. Set the mat face down on this with half an inch exposed all around. Miter the corners and fold the four edges over the board, then press flat. Turn the mat over and press the surface smooth.

Trays with Card Decorations

Trays of all kinds provide another way to use our Christmas cards. This suggestion from Roxanno Wester-meyer can be carried out by combining cutouts from cards with pressed leaves or grasses. Glue pieces on the tray and coat the surface with one of the resin products such as Hyplar and Natcol Poly Coat. A pretty festive tray is always a welcome gift.

Baskets of Cones
(Illustration 21)

For another simple and decorative gift, I select several different kinds of cones and arrange them in a basket to display—mainly through contrast—their color, shape and texture. Flat baskets allow the cones to be seen easily. Bits of lichen add another texture. This is a pleasant means of using some of your finest cones in an informal manner.

To decorate the handle of the basket shown, I included a wooden bird, plainly carved. These birds are available from Mountain Meadow Enterprises in different designs. See "Sources of Supplies" for the listing.

A Lighted Star
(Illustration 22)

One of our loveliest Christmas traditions is the lighted star. I have made this one of small rust-colored cones, a species of leucadendron, and small white lights on a raised, 1-inch-high wire frame. The frame would fit into a 20-inch circle. The star is outlined with a string of 30 lights, 6 on each point. A florist can usually order star-shaped frames from a wire-frame wholesaler for you.

I first covered the frame with lightweight metal foil—

68

ILLUSTRATION 21
BASKET OF CONES. An attractive basket with a variety of cones, casually arranged, is a welcome gift. A hand-carved bird decorates the handle.

69

ILLUSTRATION 22

A LIGHTED STAR. Small rust-colored cones, a species of leucadendron, are attached with adhesive to a foil-covered frame, outlined with little lights.

it is easy to shape foil and it gives a surface for an adhesive. Then I made a pattern of the star and from it cut out a piece of $\frac{1}{4}$-inch-mesh hardware cloth which I attached to the frame with No. 28 wire.

The ruffly cones are held in place with a sticky slow-drying adhesive, Garland Ceramic-Tile Cement, first colored with enough burnt sienna tinting color to match the brown of the cones.

I also colored the sockets on the string of lights with a material used to paint plastic models, Wood Tan pactra Namel (available at hobby and Sprouse Reitz stores). This makes them inconspicuous. The cord can be painted, too, to match a wall or door.

To install the lights I pressed three evenly spaced holes through the metal foil on each side of the points. With tapered, long-nosed pliers I eased the mesh open to the size needed for the sockets. Then, placing the star face down, I attached the lights from inside the star, beginning with the one nearest the plug. Tape holds the extra lengths of cord between lights to the back of the frame.

The hanger is the next consideration. On the point opposite the cord I fastened the middle of a 12-inch length of wire to the frame, leaving two 6-inch wires to put through a hole in the backing.

I traced the outline of the star on a piece of heavy brown posterboard, cut it out, and made two holes with an awl on each side of the five points. I also made a separate hole for the two wires for hanging the star, and then laid the cardboard on the back of the star and pulled the wires through. The cardboard is held with wires put through the holes around the wire of the frame, with ends twisted to make it firm. I used a curved needle, but it is easy enough to put the wires through the holes without one. With the backing in place, I fastened a ring to the two wires for hanging, and covered the edges of the star with bits of soft green moss.

3. Arrangements Outdoors

Ornaments of pods and cones, pebbles, shells, and driftwood need not remain indoors. Now that resin is available and there are several other products that protect natural materials from dampness, we can design decorations for our outdoor living areas, too. Mobiles and plaques can hang in a patio, and garden walls, arbors, and fences can be enhanced with all manner of treasures from our collections. A protective layer of resin, poured over materials and frames, keeps moisture from spoiling their freshness, and you can wipe the decorations occasionally with a damp cloth to keep them clean and sparkling.

In this chapter I describe some of the ornaments I made for our own garden, and elsewhere in the book you will find ideas for decorations suited to your garden or terrace. A birdhouse covered with flat stones (Illustration 64) or a rock-decorated planter (Illustration 63) might be appropriate.

Working with Resin

A whole new area of design has been opened up in recent years with the availability of plastics. Artists, scientists, and engineers have been experimenting with plastics for over a decade, and now, in California and elsewhere, hobby shops, art schools, and adult education departments are offering classes in how to use plastics. Formerly plastics were obtainable for commercial use primarily, but now hardware stores, art supply stores, hobby shops, and even dime stores stock them.

Resin is a clear liquid plastic which hardens when mixed with a catalyst. It comes in many combinations for different uses. Follow directions on the can for mixing and applying. I have found two booklets, *Casting in Clear Plastic* and *Liquid Plastic Artistry,* which provide simple basic instructions. They are available from Natcol Laboratories which also has supplies and accessories for working with resin. (See "Sources of Supplies" for address.)

Because the field is vast—and changing every day—I am limiting my comments here to a few basic procedures you may find helpful in making a particular project.

My Basic Procedure

Having my work area planned out and all materials on hand before starting is my first essential. I set up a perfectly level table *out of doors* to avoid inhaling fumes, and cover it with a sheet of mylar—a stiff, flexible material available in any hobby shop that sells plastic supplies. Resin does not stick to it. You can also use metal foil for the same purpose, but for large projects, mylar is more satisfactory. If you work on a board, it should be somewhat larger than the decoration so you can move the completed project into the sun to dry.

Materials for working with resin include: a can of resin and the accompanying bottle of hardener (the catalyst); a smooth stick for stirring such as a popsicle stick, or a small paintbrush; unwaxed paper cups with a half-cup level marked on them, or a regular measuring cup; plastic spoons to catch the drips after pouring the resin needed; a detergent such as Boraxo mixed with hot water for washing your hands; a roll of paper towels; and acetone.

Note: Resin must not be inhaled or left on your hands. I wash my hands with Boraxo detergent and hot water frequently while working on a project.

I use paper cups for mixing the resin and hardener, but

you can use a measuring cup and clean it with acetone or detergent and hot water. Follow the instructions on the can of resin, figuring out the number of drops of hardener for a half-cup. In hot weather, resin hardens noticeably faster, so I then use a smaller amount of the catalyst than at other times.

In a number of designs in this book I have applied a coating of resin both to bring up the color of materials and to provide a protective layer. The resin surface can be wiped with a damp cloth or brush to keep dust and dirt from dulling.

Rattan Frames and Resin

To use resin with rattan frames, you first need to make a backing for the frame, cut to the exact shape and thoroughly sealed with glue. As an added precaution, cover the outer seams with narrow masking tape to be sure no resin leaks through. If any does, however, it can be removed with a knife before it has hardened. Take the masking tape off as soon as the resin has set.

Various backing materials can be used. Mylar is stiff and flexible, and the resin does not adhere to it; this allows you to remove the mylar from the frame after the resin has set but before it has hardened completely. Cut

76

the mylar a little larger than the outline of the frame, glue it to all sections of the rattan, then trim with a razor blade to the edge and seal with masking tape.

With picture frames I have used fiberglass, plexiglass, and ordinary ribbed glass as permanent backing material. Plexiglass is an ideal surface for this purpose as the resin adheres closely to it, and it is more compatible than glass which may crack if completely coated with resin.

An Outdoor Display
(Illustration 23)

Our garden is under a fine old madrone tree (*Arbutus menzesii*) with branches reaching 100 feet and a trunk 7 feet in diameter. In summer the lovely pinkish-tan leaves fall to the ground and the rust-colored bark peels off in large curling sheets, exposing clean yellow-green limbs. Leaves and bark make the spectacular carpet shown in the photograph.

To break up a long fenced backyard and give depth to the garden as well as privacy for a work area, our landscape architect designed screens of marine plywood, with sections approximately 3 by 4 feet, framed with lengths of surfaced redwood, 2 by 6 inches. These screens stand about 10 inches off the ground in staggered units.

77

ILLUSTRATION 23

SCREENED GARDEN. Plywood panels framed with redwood give depth and privacy to our backyard. Leaves embedded in plastic and a tree of pods and cones enhance the view from the patio.

The one on the right has two sections, the middle three, and one at the left (not shown) is also a three-sectioned screen. All are painted a soft brown.

Each screen has a different decoration: plexiglass panels with pressed ferns and leaves; a tree of pods, cones, berries, and lichen wired to hardware cloth; and rattan frames with pebbles, shells, and glass rings and dried flowers. The plexiglass panels are set into the plywood while the tree and rattan frames are wired through holes. Decorations are coated with resin except the tree of pods, cones, and berries, which is sprayed with Thompson's Water Seal.

Pressed Leaves on Plexiglass Panels
(Illustration 23 and Color Illustration 6)

Sunlight is part of this design. In the early part of the day it shines directly on the leaves, making them radiant with color; later, it places them in silhouette, making outlines important. The plexiglass panels are 10 by 50 inches.

To make these panels I first glued brightly colored pressed leaves and ferns on the plexiglass, overlapping in some areas, leaving spaces in others. (Directions for pressing leaves are given in Chapter 6.) Then I laid the panel on a sheet of mylar and poured resin mixed with

79

a few drops of hardener by the half-cupful over the leaves. When the resin had dried I added successive coats to give a wavy depth—an effect I prefer to a flat manufactured-looking surface.

Tree of Pods, Cones, and Berries
(Illustration 23 and Color Illustration 5)

The central panel of this three-sectioned screen has a bas-relief tree of pods and cones large enough to be effective from a distance. On a 3- by 4-foot piece of heavy half-inch-mesh hardware cloth I sketched with chalk a general outline for the tree. Using a great variety of large pieces, each with a single wire attached, I began placing material along a center line and worked outward. I let the tree develop in a naturalistic vein, keeping in mind contrast in texture, size, and color so each piece would be clearly defined. Chartreuse staghorn lichen from the trees of the Sierra Nevada Mountains is worked in among the pods and cones. With a paper pattern to guide the shape, I sawed out a trunk of yellow pine bark and attached it to the plywood with screws. Small pieces of bark glued over the screw heads conceal them.

After materials were wired in place I trimmed most

of the hardware cloth to the outline, but left some of the wires to pull through holes drilled in the plywood backing. Since resin does not adhere for more than a year to pods that have a certain kind of natural finish (bottle tree, lotus, and carob pods), I used a more penetrating material, Floral Preservative. Thompson's Water Seal in spray form is also an effective coating for plant material exposed to dampness, and you can put an acrylic spray on top, if you wish.

To mount the tree I pulled the wires through the holes in the plywood and wound them around screws on the reverse side.

Rattan Frames for Outdoor Panels
(Illustrations 24, 25, and 26)

Three different frames decorate a screen of three sections placed to the left of the Japanese maple in Illustration 23. These are on the opposite side of the yard from the leaf transparencies.

The frames were first prepared with a backing of mylar attached with a ribbon of glue to every section of the frame, then trimmed with a razor blade to the edge of the frame and sealed with masking tape as described above in "Rattan Frames and Resin."

81

ILLUSTRATION 24
RATTAN WREATH. Pebbles and rocks covered with resin decorate this 30-inch wreath which hangs on a plywood panel in the garden.

ILLUSTRATION 25
RATTAN CIRCLES. A variety of colorful shells and six African
Banksia larisina pods are embedded in resin and attached to a
panel in a plywood outdoor screen.

ILLUSTRATION 26

RATTAN FRAME WITH TINY CIRCLES. Green, gold, and red glass
and plastic rings and a golden anthemus flower embellish rattan
circles. The entire frame is filled with glasslike resin and
mounted on one of three panels in an outdoor screen.

In the 30-inch rattan wreath (Illustration 24) I first put a large rock in the center of each section. Around each rock I spread small bright pebbles. The background is filled in with smooth, flat, slate-gray Japanese stones. After placing all the material I poured resin over every piece.

Shells predominate in the rattan frame of six circles, 12 inches in diameter (Illustration 26). They are of many kinds, collected from beaches or purchased from hobby shops, garden shows, county fairs and through catalogs. In the center of each circle is a handsome sculptural pod from Africa, *Banksia larisina*. Resin covers every part, including the frame.

The rectangular frame, 17 by 36 inches, has thirty-six 4-inch circles (Illustration 26). In each of these I placed glass and plastic rings—green, gold, and red in graded sizes—and at the center a dried golden anthemus flower. Then I filled the frame with resin.

These three frames are attached to the plywood with wires passed through holes drilled in the wood and wound around screws on the reverse side. The mylar need not be removed.

Decoy Covered with Seeds and Pods
(Illustration 28)

On the patio sits this once-battered decoy now decked out with seeds and pods made shiny with a coating of resin. I had great fun selecting seeds to give the illusion of feathers. All are glued or attached with Plastico Rok adhesive.

For the beak I chose flat black yucca seeds. For the eyes I used a small scarlet seed with one black dot, *Abrus precatorius,* and a ring of green split peas. The head is covered with soft brown beechnut seeds and among the seeds are tufts of dark brown volcano grass. Around the neck and on the breast I put flat sandbox pods and large spotted castor-bean seeds. Sunflower seeds trim the sides. Sections of mahogany pods make wings and tail. On the back are flat, smooth, brown seeds of the sapodilla tree, *Achras zapota,* and chunky black seeds of the Cape chestnut, *Calodendrum capensis.* For the

---

ILLUSTRATION 27

DRIFTWOOD PANEL. A weathered board, Monterey pine cones, and a dried branch of liquidambar with corklike formations hang on the patio wall. Materials are attached with Plastico Rok adhesive.

ILLUSTRATION 28

A Duck for the Patio. Seeds and pods coated with resin disguise a battered decoy.

underside of the body I used buff-colored sea oats, *Uniola latifolia.*

When this was accomplished I felt some legs were in order, to raise the body up a little, and found in my barrel of driftwood a looped branch with a root that suggested a swimming duck's foot. I attached this with a little Plastico Rok, gave the completed duck a coating of resin, and placed it on a polished free-form slab of walnut.

4. House Decorations and Gifts

In this chapter I describe ideas for gifts, for fairs and bazaars, and for decorations to enhance your own home. Most of the suggestions are simple to assemble. I have not given detailed instructions here. Pressed leaves, for example, are discussed fully in Chapter 6 and ways with shells in Chapter 7. What you use to embellish a lampshade or a pair of bookends will depend on what you have at hand. Here are ways to create attractive objects by combining things from nature with manufactured items—light switches with shells or seeds; matchboxes with dried leaves, flowers, and mosses; an electric clock with seeds and pods. This hobby, so much in keeping with the current trend to handmade furnishings and accessories, can be a creative outlet with useful results.

Sculpture in a Setting
(Illustration 29)

Sculpture in an appropriate setting of natural materials can be a source of continuing pleasure in our homes. I have been enjoying a figure of St. Francis sculpted by Will Forni of formulated stone and volcanic rock from the San Andreas fault. For this saint I made an environment of driftwood and moss-covered rocks on a metal lazy-susan stand. One of nature's sculptures, the twist of wood on the right, holds black pottery birds from Mexico. A dried branch of St. Catherine's lace (*Eriogonum giganteum*), indigenous to Catalina Island, suggests a tree. The branch is supported by clay between the rocks behind the figure.

The acid-treated stone and textured surfaces of the Forni sculpture associate well with natural materials. In "Sources of Supplies" I have listed the location of the studio.

Ball of Piñon Scales
(Illustration 30)

If you place piñon cones in a slow oven, not more than 200 degrees F., until the dull waxy pitch melts, the tan, rough-textured scales emerge with shining green tips. The scales can be removed from the cones and used for various ornaments. Piñon cones come from the only single-needled pine, *Pinus monophylla*, which grows west of the Rockies. The seed of the piñon pine has a soft delicious kernel—it is marketed today and has always been harvested by the Indians as a source of food.

This hollow fiberboard ball, 10 inches in diameter,

is decorated with scales attached with Plastico Rok adhesive. Ceramic-tile cement can be used as well if first colored with burnt sienna tinting color. After pulling the cones apart—use garden clippers or pliers—I trimmed the ragged ends of the scales to make them fit neatly, and sorted the scales according to size. The ball (available from hobby shops) has a line marking the middle section. I started attaching large scales above the line and worked upward, gradually decreasing the size of the scales. Each is fitted under the one below. Then I turned the ball over and repeated the procedure for the lower half. Frequently I had to trim the ends a second time to make them join properly. Very small scales are at the top and bottom.

Before finishing the top, I devised a hanger. I wrapped a strong wire about 4 inches long around the middle of a thin 3-inch nail. Then I made a slit in the center of the top of the ball with a sharp knife, slipped the nail inside and turned it at right angles to the opening, with the end of the wire remaining out of the ball. The slit

---

ILLUSTRATION 29

St. Francis. Driftwood and moss-covered rocks on a revolving pedestal make the base for this nature-loving saint. A branch of St. Catherine's lace suggests a tree.

was patched with Mystic tape and adhesive and covered with small scales.

The band around the middle is filled with rosettes that grow at the stem end of the piñon cone, trimmed to match, and fitted closely together.

The orange-winged butterfly was assembled by wiring together two sections of dragon-tree leaves (*Dracaena draco*) with a screw bean glued on for the body. The flared orange section grows at the base of the leaf where it joins the branch. A dab of Plastico Rok holds the butterfly on the scales.

When the ball was completed, I hung it from a chain looped over a rattan hook. A brass ring or cord could be substituted for the chain.

Although no finish was needed for decorative purposes, I sprayed a thin protective coating of Floral Spray wax on both the ball and butterfly.

ILLUSTRATION 30

SHINING BALL. Scales of piñon cones, heated in a slow oven to melt the pitch, are fitted to a fiberboard ball to make this attractive decoration for an informal room.

Decorated Clock
(Illustration 31)

To make a frame for an electric wall clock, I selected red-brown protea pods and flaky seeds from casuarina (*Casuarina stricta*) cones—the largest of many varieties. Around the edge I glued a braid of natural fiber, stained brown.

I used Plastico Rok adhesive to build up the flower-like pods rather than attach them directly with glue. When the adhesive was hard I removed each pod with its base from the smooth enamel surface and glued it back on. (Plastico Rok does not adhere firmly to smooth surfaces.)

I arranged seeds with the aid of tweezers and a tube of transparent glue, covering all exposed areas of the enameled rim, and finished the edge with braid glued in place.

Lampshade with Seeds
(Illustration 32)

A plain white lampshade can be made much more attractive with delicate seeds, leaves, and choice items in your collection. For this one I first traced the outlines of actual leaves at intervals around the shade, then

ILLUSTRATION 31

CLOCK DECORATED WITH SEEDS AND PODS. An electric wall clock is given an ornamental frame of rust-colored protea pods and flaky seeds, edged with a natural fiber braid, stained brown.

ILLUSTRATION 32

LAMPSHADE. Leaf designs of red-brown casuarina seeds, combined with an overall pattern of tulip-tree seeds, enliven a plain white shade. A braid of raffia, also reddish brown, trims top and bottom.

applied transparent glue directly from the tube and filled in the leaf designs on the shade with reddish-brown casuarina seeds. The rest of the shade is covered with filmy seeds found in the boat-shaped pods of the tulip tree (*Spathodea campanulata*), also attached with transparent glue applied to the hard center of the seeds. Overlapping made the iridescent part of the seeds project a little. A braid of red-brown raffia is glued to the top and bottom of the shade with a fringe of seeds.

Light-switch Plates
(Illustration 33)

To make plastic light-switch plates into pleasing ornaments, glue on seeds, shells, or grasses in attractive patterns and brush lightly with a protective layer of resin such as Natcol Poly Coat (see "Sources of Supplies"). I have developed three designs, each in a different style, to suggest possible combinations. You can use the switch plates as accents or let them blend in with the color of the wall. On the left, layers of dried squash seeds painted gold; in the middle, sea oats; and on the right, delicate orange shells collected on a California beach during an early morning walk. These shells were found attached to long strands of kelp and some had pink barnacles growing on them.

ILLUSTRATION 33

ORNAMENTAL LIGHT-SWITCH PLATES. With seeds, grasses, and shells, plastic switch-plates can be transformed into pretty additions to a room.

The seeds are from small, hard, green squash. Scoop them out with a strong spoon, strip off the pulp and rinse in a colander. Then let them dry out *thoroughly* on waxed paper before storing—otherwise they may mold.

Miniatures for a Child's Room
(Illustration 34)

Lois Walker has devised appealing arrangements of tiny pods, cones, dried flowers, and grasses combined with little figures for decorations in a child's room. The materials are glued to 2-inch glass rings and mounted (*top*) on mahogany veneer neatly trimmed with half-inch-wide green velvet ribbon. In the lower picture the rings are placed on a 3-inch width of matching velvet ribbon glued to veneer. Note the figures' cunning hats: one is a cap from a eucalyptus pod; another a pussy-willow tuft suggesting fur; and two sport berets of scalloped, ridged caps that are found on Oriental poppy pods. Here, indeed, is an imaginative use of natural materials.

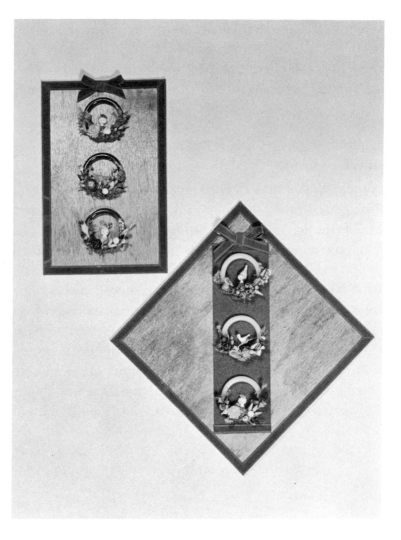

Fireplace Screen
(Illustration 35)

When the season for fires is past, this screen of cones bordered with bunya-bunya scales is an attractive decoration for the empty hearth. Mrs. Vernon Behel designed this screen to fit the opening of her fireplace. She made two wooden frames the same size, placed heavy hardware cloth between and nailed the frames together. Then she coated mesh and frame with a copper spray.

The crescent shape was first outlined with the handsome *Araucaria bidwillii* scales, then filled in with cones and tufts of yellow-green staghorn lichen. Cones and scales were prepared with wires and attached directly to the mesh. (Basic wiring directions are given in Chapter 1, and the specific instructions are described in Chapter 2 for a Fan of Large Cones, (Illustration 17.)

———————————

ILLUSTRATION 34
DESIGNS IN MINIATURE. Mahogany veneer, framed with green velvet, is the background for miniature birds and figures perched on glass rings in settings of tiny pods, cones, flowers, and grasses. Lois Walker made these delightful designs to decorate a child's room.

ILLUSTRATION 35

FIRESCREEN FOR SUMMER. A crescent of cones and bunya-bunya scales interspersed with tufts of lichen is wired to heavy hardware cloth to provide a decorative screen for an unused hearth. This one was designed by Mrs. Vernon Behel.

104

Candle Centerpiece
(Color Illustration 11)

Attractive centerpieces can be made with large candles on decorative bases of colorful dried flowers, pressed leaves, dainty shells, and other small objects. This one is made on a circle of masonite, 8 inches in diameter. Large pink and white acrocliniums, golden dwarf marigolds, large yellow acacia balls, green soapbark tree pods (*Quillaja saponaria*), lavender-pink xeranthemums, and a border of pink gomphrena are glued to the board, and sphagnum moss trims the edge.

To make the lei I glued moss and a few yellow acacia balls to flexible gold ribbon and attached the lei to the candle with a tapelike clay called Vogue Stickum. Pink glass birds and rosy-red pressed leaves are included among the dried flowers.

Strawflower Bouquets
(Illustration 36)

Bright strawflowers make cheerful, lasting arrangements. Lois Walker made these attractive ornaments with strawflowers from her garden. Stems were replaced with short wires immediately after cutting (see directions in Chapter 1 for Strawflower Tree, Color Illustration 9),

ILLUSTRATION 36

STRAWFLOWER BOUQUETS. Wired strawflowers placed in sections
of Styrofoam balls in pretty vases make colorful, lasting arrangements. Lois Walker designed these charming examples.

and flowers allowed to dry. The wires are inserted into sections of Styrofoam balls, carved to fit into vases. These colorful arrangements make effective winter decorations and are wonderful hospital gifts.

Pine-cone Pineapples
(Illustration 37)

The idea for constructing pineapples of pods and cones was passed on to me by a friend who had seen them in Hawaii. Since Jeffrey cones grow to be 6 inches high and already suggest the shape of a pineapple, these seemed a logical choice. I selected cones with widely separated scales and where the scales were too close I removed them with long-nosed pliers. Pods with a cross design on the flat end—blue gum (*Eucalyptus globulus*) —create the pineapple effect. This design varies from tree to tree, and it is best to select one kind of blue-gum pod for each pineapple.

When I could wedge a pod in tightly between the scales I used glue to hold it; otherwise I applied sticky ceramic-tile cement to hold it firm. Long-nosed pliers were a help in setting pods in place.

I trimmed stiff watsonia leaves to the length I wanted, tucked the ends down in the top of the cone, and

ILLUSTRATION 37

PINE-CONE PINEAPPLES. Blue-gum pods inserted between scales of
Jeffrey cones make distinctive pineapples with watsonia leaves
as tops. They can be arranged with carved wooden fruit in a
basket tray or, without leaves, serve as candleholders.

108

squeezed glue on directly from the tube. Tops could be made of New Zealand flax leaves, too.

For a soft finish I sprayed the pineapples with Floral Spray.

Pine-cone Pineapple Ornaments for the Wall

Helen Young suggested that the pine-cone pineapple might be adapted for a wall decoration. Saw Jeffrey pine cones in half lengthwise and make the pineapples with blue-gum pods and watsonia leaves, following the procedure described above. After the pods are secured, cut out a backing of cardboard or heavy felt and attach it with glue or Plastico Rok adhesive. Then determine the angle for hanging the pineapple and attach a hanger to the backing.

You could also make an attractive wall plaque by mounting one of these half-pineapples on a slab of polished wood.

Decorated Matchboxes
(Illustration 38)

Tall boxes of matches for the fireplace are suited to modest decorations of small cones, pods, leaves, and dried flowers. These boxes from gift shops are usually covered with interesting papers and need only the addition of

a few well-chosen materials to make them one-of-a-kind. Here, against an overall pattern of green with gold tracery, three deep red pods of *Eucalyptus erythrocorys* are grouped with prickly-edged leaves from a strawberry tree, *Arbutus unedo,* picked when autumn-red. These are attached to the box with glue and adhesive. Glued to the bottom of the box is a square of cardboard slightly larger than the box, decorated with clusters of dark green eucalyptus pods. A cluster of the same pods is glued to the top of the box. This is a good bazaar item.

Bookends
(Illustration 39)

To decorate a pair of workaday metal bookends I first cut out pieces of flat and soft cajeput bark, *Melaleuca leucadendron,* and glued them to the upright sections. Then to keep the bookends from scratching a surface, I applied adhesive-backed brown felt to the underneath side of the horizontal supports.

For the bookend shown on the left I have used

ILLUSTRATION 38
FIRESIDE MATCHES. For a gift or bazaar item, tall boxes of matches covered with unusual papers can be embellished quickly with leaves and pods.

ILLUSTRATION 39

BOOKENDS. Plain metal bookends have been made into attractive gifts with colorful pressed leaves and pods on a background of cajeput bark.

pressed yellow ginkgo leaves and a group of three eucalyptus pods with a chinaberry and open beechnut cone.
The edging is made of dry acacia balls. On the right are
pressed pelargonium leaves and a cluster of *Eucalyptus
lehmannii* 'Max Watson' pods, with center caps removed. The edge is trimmed with beechnut seeds. Heavier materials are held with Plastico Rok adhesive, and
leaves and seeds with glue. I brushed liquid plastic wax
on seeds, leaves, and pods.

Bookends of wood can be decorated effectively with
any natural materials of suitable size.

Matchboxes and Place Cards
(Illustration 40)

A charming gift and a delight for your own use are
little matchboxes and place cards embellished with small
choice pieces of moss, dried flowers, cones, and tiny
pods. Making these is a continuing pleasure of mine.

You can cover the matchboxes with any number of
materials. I have used natural wood veneer paper and
fiber cloth in the ones shown, and the place cards are
made of wood veneer. (See "Sources of Supplies.") All
materials suited to these little objects can be attached
with transparent glue.

For a new effect I mixed one cup of maple varnish-

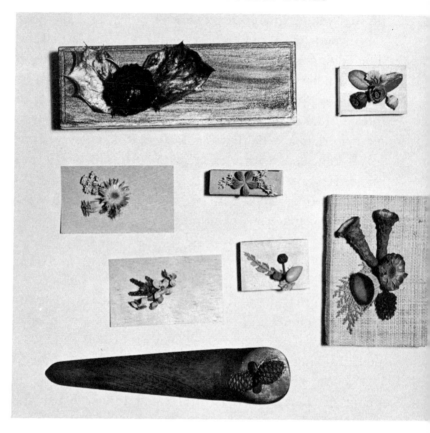

ILLUSTRATION 40

IN MINIATURE. Matchboxes, place cards, and a paper cutter are transformed with choice bits of moss, tiny pods, flowers, and cones. Natural veneer papers make a suitable background.

stain, one cup of turpentine, and a tablespoon (or more) of gold powder. This is painted on the flat wooden box shown at the top left of the photograph. Since the gold tends to settle, if you keep stirring the mixture with the brush, you get an unusual streaked effect. Natural materials painted with this mixture resemble metal sculpture. The two mahonia leaves on the box are painted with the gold mixture and the cone is also.

Small baskets of pods and cones on short, wrapped wires, perhaps cut to resemble flowers, can be treated with this solution, as can the baskets.

5. Ornaments for the Wall

Making decorations to hang on a wall is an area for infinite experimentation. I have made suggestions in this chapter that use rattan frames as they are, or sprayed with color, some with backings of cardboard or transparent mylar for seed mosaics; framed plexiglass as a background for pods and seeds with a coating of resin; a hanging of cork with fiber mats; a cabinet door with a tree of pods and cones; Victorian frames; plaques for simple display of beautiful pods. All will hopefully stimulate you to imaginative endeavors. Look at standard accessories with an eye to using them in a new way—as I have done with a teakwood stand in Illustration 43. And try all sorts of combinations. Often what seems unlikely at first yields exciting results.

Rattan Rooster with Seeds
(Illustration 41)

A rattan frame of a crowing rooster suggested a colorful project using shiny bright seeds and featherlike grasses. If framed, the dimensions would be about 20 inches square. I cut lightweight brown cardboard to fill the open sections—the body, wing, and foot—and glued it to the back of the rattan.

With transparent glue I attached red false wiliwili seeds (*Adenanthera pavonina*) to the woven part for comb and wattle, round black seeds from the papery pods of the goldenrain or Chinese lantern tree (*Koelreuteria paniculata*) for the beak, and a small orange love apple (*Solanum aculeatissimum*) for the eye. Beechnut seeds, smooth and brown, form the body of the rooster. They are attached to the cardboard with Plastico Rok adhesive. The wing is made of small prickly cones (*Casuarina cunninghamiana*), and the small section under the tail has reddish-brown kernels of Indian corn, also attached with Plastico Rok. For feathers, I tucked pointed tufts of russet Hawaiian volcano grass (*Cladium meyenii*) between the seeds, after they were in place, using transparent glue. The tail is trimmed with wiry curls of a grass from Australia called caustiz commercially, also glued to the rattan. Golden kernels of Indian corn fill the foot area.

A plant preservative was sprayed over the design to brighten the materials and keep them looking fresh. (See Chapter 1 for "Note on Plant Preservatives.") A simple loop of wire attached to a section of the rattan serves as a hanger.

Butterfly
(Color Illustration 13)

For this rattan frame, a little less than 12 inches across, I made a backing of transparent, flexible mylar. You can use cellophane, but it is not as firm as mylar.

Lay the frame on a sheet of mylar and with a razor blade or scissors cut out a piece about a half-inch larger than the outline of the frame. Apply a continuous ribbon of glue around the underside of the frame and press it on the mylar, sealing it well so that when the resin is poured, it will not leak through. Then trim off the excess mylar with a razor blade (a close edge is important here), and apply a thin strip of masking tape around the frame to insure a good seal. This tape is removed later after the design is completed, but before the resin has hardened completely.

I selected seeds and glued them to the mylar. The outer wing sections have an edging of red seeds from the bean-shaped pods of a species of coral tree (*Erythrina*), and tiny red *Abrus precatorius* seeds in the middle.

ILLUSTRATION 41
Rooster. Seeds and grasses embellish this lively rattan rooster frame.

Eyes in the feelers are these same small seeds turned to show the black dot on one end of the seed. The gold section of the wing is made with yellow split peas, and shiny gray Job's tears (*Coix lacryma-jobi*) fill the rounded sections next to the body. The body itself is of flat black seeds of New Zealand flax, with a row of patterned pods of the Australian tea tree (*Leptospermum laevigatum*) down the middle. Black-centered brown seeds from the earpod tree (*Enterlobium cyclocarpum*) are used in the lower sections. Individual seeds in the rattan coils are four loquat seeds, two black seeds from the goldenrain tree, and two red false wiliwili seeds. Of course, many other kinds of seeds can be used.

After the seeds were set I put the butterfly on a level surface on a piece of metal foil or mylar (resin does not stick to either one) and poured on the liquid resin mixed with a catalyst, smoothing it with a soft paintbrush on the rattan. Resin brightens the colors and provides a durable surface that does not attract dust and can be cleaned with a damp brush. (See "Working with Resin" in Chapter 3.)

To hang up the butterfly I drilled a hole straight across the feelers, put a wire through and made a loop on the back. A small nail beside the edge of the wing holds the butterfly at any angle.

Rattan Leaf Mosaics
(Color Illustration 14)

These three leaves are assembled in much the same manner as the preceding Butterfly (Color Illustration 13). A backing of flat, stiff mylar was made first, cut out a little larger than the frames and attached to the rattan with a continuous strip of glue. After trimming the mylar with a razor blade to the edge of the frames, I added strips of masking tape to make sure that when the resin was poured there would be no place where it might seep through. (The tape is removed just before the resin dries.)

Using transparent glue, I filled each section of the leaf forms with bright seeds, cones, and pods. The top leaf has red and green seeds, the one on the left has black, brown, and golden seeds, and the leaf on the right is filled with a great assortment of small pods and cones and even a few dried yellow statice blossoms. I placed the completed leaves on a level table on top of a piece of foil and poured resin into each section to cover the seeds.

To hang these leaves up, I wrapped fine wire around the stem next to the leaf sections and looped it at the back.

Rattan Ornament
(Illustration 42)

Some of the rattan backgrounds are so airy and open I feel they should remain that way with only a few pieces of material for color and accent. They make charming wall ornaments. These backgrounds can also be decorated on both sides and suspended by a length of strong thread to twist slowly in a breeze, or hung by four wires, face down, high in a room from a hook in a beamed ceiling.

This 24-inch rattan frame is embellished with stems of bead grass glued between the straight pieces, bright red false wiliwili seeds also glued in the center of each coil, and a flower-like brown *Protea mellifera* pod in the middle. The pod was fastened to a circle of cardboard with Plastico Rok adhesive and the cardboard wired to the frame.

ILLUSTRATION 42

CIRCULAR RATTAN ORNAMENT. Red false wiliwili seeds are glued to each coil; stems of dark brown bead grass and a dramatic protea pod trim this pretty 24-inch rattan frame.

Topiary Tree
(Illustration 43)

This wall decoration is made on the *underside* of a 7- by 14-inch teakwood stand, the kind used for a base in flower arrangements and available from gift and import shops, Sears garden departments, and florists. By inverting the stand I had a plaque that looks like a scroll.

I first sketched the three graded oval shapes and the flower pot on paper. Then I cut them out and drew the outlines with chalk on the teak. With fine sandpaper I carefully rubbed each area so the adhesive for the pods could penetrate the wood and hold them firm. This material is mounted with Plastico Rok which builds it up from the wood. For a flat tree you would use glue.

I attached a wide assortment of pods, caps, and flowers of a species of eucalyptus, ranging from gray and green to warm red-brown. The trunk is of long caps of *Eucalyptus lehmannii,* but pieces of branch could be used

---

ILLUSTRATION 43

Topiary Tree. Tiny pods, caps, and flowers of a species of eucalyptus are mounted with Plastico Rok adhesive on the underside of a scrolled teakwood stand.

instead. The container is of one kind of pod. I gathered them when green and dried them in the dark to keep their color, which sets off those in the tree to advantage.

I am lucky enough to have access to a garden of 250 species of eucalyptus where I may gather caps, pods, and flowers. Seasonal changes in fruits yield a variety of forms, and blossoms dry with good color. If you do not live in an area where you can collect these fascinating pods, they are available in kits. (See "Sources of Supplies.")

Eucalyptus Pods Make a Tree
(Illustration 44)

A 12- by 18-inch frame and backing of natural wood seemed a suitable means of displaying the varied shapes, sizes, colors, and textures of eucalyptus pods. I made this tree of green, tan, brown, and gray pods with a slab of eucalyptus bark for the trunk. You can use any kind of pod-and-cone collection that has sufficient variety.

Draw the tree shape on paper, cut it out, trace with

ILLUSTRATION 44

Framed Tree of Eucalyptus Pods. Contrasting shapes, colors, and textures give variety to this tree of pods attached with Plastico Rok to a framed backing of natural wood.

chalk onto the background. If the wood has a finish, sand the area where the pods will go so the adhesive can penetrate and hold. Plastico Rok is a little like modeling clay and with it pods can be built out from the surface in a compact design. For a flat effect, use glue. After the tree is completed you may want to brush the pods with a floral preservative to bring up the colors and give them a fresh look.

Tree on a Door
(Illustration 45)

An excellent source for ready-made backgrounds is a cabinet shop. Shirley Stephens has made use of this source in constructing a delightful tree of handsomely matched pods and cones. This tall, narrow door panel has natural stain with soft green on the molding frame. First a paper pattern was drawn, cut out, then laid on a piece of screening or fine woven hardware cloth, which makes a better surface for attaching pods than the wood. This was cut out and tacked down on the wood. Then

---

ILLUSTRATION 45

TREE ON A DOOR. To make this handsome tree, Shirley Stephens used a cabinet door for the background, and attached pods and cones to hardware cloth tacked to the wood.

pods and cones were attached with very thick linoleum paste or a ceramic-tile cement. As a finishing touch, yellow-green Sierra lichen was tucked between the pods and around the edge of the tree.

Red Berry Tree in a Frame
(Color Illustration 4)

In a shop that sells plastics you can frequently come across pieces left from larger sections. This is how I found the plexiglass which I had framed to use as a backing for this tree of red Brazilian pepper berries (*Schinus terebinthifolius*).

Two green glass bracelets, one inside the other with green and gold glass chips in the center, are placed to suggest a base for the tree. Above is a large beetle with a shimmering, opalescent back and two okra pods are on either side of the trunk. A flock of small glass birds perches on the branches.

I attached all materials to the plexiglass with transparent glue. Then I poured resin to cover all parts but not submerge them. (See instructions in Chapter 3, "Working with Resin.")

The picture is hung on a straight wire stretched between two small screws across the top of the frame to conceal the wire.

Victorian Frames
(Illustrations 46 and 47)

For decorations with a Victorian air, oval frames with convex glass can be effective with dried but not necessarily pressed material. Because there is ample room between the glass and backing, bulkier pods, berries, flowers, and such can be used. In one frame, large golden-brown *Protea mellifera* pods are associated with brown grasses—the curly one from Australia is called caustiz (a commercial name), and the other is probably swamp cane. All are glued to a backing of grasscloth.

In another frame I have mounted a yellow-green sea-fan with blue on a neutral background, and decorated it with golden anthemus flowers, four fringed flowering pods of *Eucalyptus preissiana,* a cream-colored double hollyhock (all dried in silica gel), and soft golden acacia balls that dried naturally.

Abaca-fiber Rosettes
(Illustration 48)

Sheet cork can be used for a textured backing for wall ornaments. On this strip, 30 inches long and 2½ inches wide, I have wired five reddish-gold mats of woven abaca fiber. Wires were put into the cork from the back

131

ILLUSTRATIONS 46 and 47

VICTORIAN DECORATIONS. Old frames with convex glass permit use of pods and other materials that are not pressed flat.

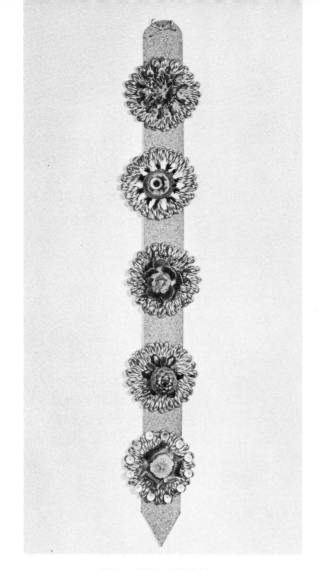

ILLUSTRATION 48
A STUDY IN TEXTURES. Woven abaca-fiber mats are wired to a
strip of cork and decorated with pods and seeds.

through holes made with an awl and directly through each mat. Then the ends were joined on top of the mat and pressed flat. The wires are concealed by the pods and cones. Glue or Plastico Rok holds the mats flat against the cork. Each mat is the background for a different flower form; the larger pods are held with Plastico Rok, the smaller with glue. The hanger at the top is a piece of gold cord inserted through two holes and tied in a bow.

The materials are identified below. Top: a center of *Leucadendron plumosum,* with beechnut seeds and pussywillow tufts. Second from top: a *Eucalyptus macrocarpa* pod with open end of a cap of *Eucalyptus lehmannii* in the center, and an edging of sea oats and volcano grass. Center: a *Banksia larisina* pod, fringed with curly caustiz grass. Second from bottom: a tropical palm edged with *Achras zapota* seeds alternated with *Casuarina cunninghamiana* cones. Bottom: a coco palm calyx with eucalyptus caps.

A Child's Decoration
(Illustration 49)

A devoted collector, Mrs. Lillian McBride, sends me boxes of intriguing treasures from the northwestern region of this country surrounding Spokane. One of her exciting contributions was a stiff, silvery lichen with a gray back and curled edges that grows on rocks along with a feathery green moss. I have used it in this whimsical ornament, designed to please a child.

Inspiration for the arrangement came from a magazine clipping. The candelabra-like frame of half-inch-square strips was one I had had made some time before putting the ornament together. I laid it on a table in my studio and placed lichen and some of my small creatures, a few at a time, until I arrived at a combination I liked. Then I glued the delicate pieces with transparent glue from a tube and secured the larger ones with Plastico Rok.

My original plan was to stand the candelabra on a base of driftwood, making a hole in the wood and adding Plastico Rok, but I decided to use it as a wall decoration instead to keep it out of reach of little fingers.

Cedar Shake Plaque
(Illustration 50)

Interesting in its irregularity, this slightly curved cedar shake suggested an informal design. It is bordered with long-stemmed dandelions with creamy-white heads and pale sprays of an ornamental grass called sea oats (*Uniola latifolia*), both attached with transparent glue.

The extraordinary vase-shaped object below the hand-carved birds available from Mountain Meadow Industries (see "Sources of Supplies"), is from a tall saguaro cactus that grows in the Arizona desert. It was brought to me by Katherine Kitchen of Tucson who explained that these "boots" develop when the pulpy trunk is damaged and the cactus seals the entire wound with a smooth hard coating to protect the moisture within. Pygmy owls and other birds make use of these insulated, readymade nests. I attached the boot and birds to the cedar with Plastico Rok adhesive.

Pods Displayed on Plaques
(Illustration 51)

These wall decorations display pods in a simple, uncontrived manner on plaques of natural wood. Materials were attached with glue or Plastico Rok depending on their weight. Some of these pods were used in the "Treasure Tree" (Illustration 1) and in the Della Robbia wreath (Illustration 11).

ILLUSTRATION 49

FOR A CHILD'S ROOM. Little owls, frogs, bears, bugs, and butterflies perch among bits of silvery lichen and moss on a candelabra form of wood strips.

137

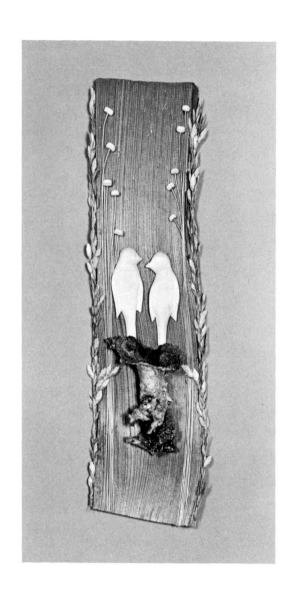

frica, and
(see listing
rmitted to
, but they
ne Division

ustralia and
macrocarpa,
Top center, a
vith rhythmic
lector tropical
ght, *Eucalyptus*
ke flowers of a
clusters of two

fish-shaped pods,
closed pod, and
seed, *Macrozamia*
ooth and grow up

50
cedar shake, edged with
sea oats, makes an un-
ot and two hand-carved

The pods shown are from Australia and Africa, and are now available in the United States in kits (see listing in "Sources of Supplies"). The traveler is permitted to bring these materials into the country, too, but they must first be inspected by the U.S. Quarantine Division and fumigated if necessary.

In the upper plaque are pods from Australia and Africa. Top left, three forms of *Eucalyptus macrocarpa*, a pod with stem, a closed pod, and a cap. Top center, a shiny, slick-surfaced, golden-brown pod with rhythmic pattern, an African pod called by the collector tropical palm. It grows to be 2½ inches. Top right, *Eucalyptus preissiana*, two pods and three brushlike flowers of a deep, golden color. These pods grow in clusters of two or three on one stem.

Near the middle of the plaque are fish-shaped pods, *Zylomelum angustifolia*, one open, one closed pod, and a seed. On their right is a deep orange seed, *Macrozamia reidlei*. These seeds are shiny and smooth and grow up to 2 inches.

ILLUSTRATION 50

CONVERSING BIRDS. The subtle curve of a cedar shake, edged with long-stemmed dandelions and sprays of sea oats, makes an unusual backing for a saguaro cactus boot and two hand-carved birds.

On the bottom row, left, are two *Banksia ericifolia* pods that combine smooth and rough surfaces; the smaller one has open sections like baby birds' beaks. Next, a ruddy pod of *Eucalyptus forestiana,* and on the right, a gray-to-brown *Banksia larisina* sculptured pod that grows to 3½ inches. In the lower plaque are pods from the Cape Province, South Africa. A *Protea mellifera* is shown top left; it is a flat, flower-like pod. Next to it, a compact round pod, *Leucadendron sabulosum,* ridged and reddish brown, about 2 inches long. Top right is a *Protea mellifera* bud on a stem, crisp and golden brown. On the bottom row, left, is a *Protea arborea,* also crisp and golden. The two pods on the right are *Leucadendron plumosum* shown in two views to reveal the pattern on the stem end. They can be cream, rust, or reddish-brown, and have silky down between each section. The sizes are up to 2 inches.

ILLUSTRATION 51

AUSTRALIAN AND AFRICAN PODS. These pods are mounted on simple plaques to exhibit their marvelous variety in shape, size, color, and texture.

6. Designing with Pressed Leaves and Resin Castings

From childhood on, the brilliant colors of autumn foliage have urged the collector in us, and at the end of a walk on a crisp fall day we find at least a few bright leaves we cannot part with. One way to continue to enjoy them is to press and dry the leaves so they retain their color, and mount them on various household objects or create picture montages. A little volume by Ruth Voorhees Booke, *Pressed Flower Pictures* has many delightful designs using pressed leaves.* I find my copy being borrowed constantly by enthusiastic students in my classes.

The simplest way to press leaves—and flowers, ferns, and grasses, too—is to lay them between the highly absorbent pages of a thick telephone book and place a heavy weight on top of it for a day or two. (If you can obtain an outdated book of wallpaper samples, use it to press leaves.) Examine leaves for any creases or folds,

* Published by D. Van Nostrand Company, Inc. (Princeton, N. J.) in 1962.

smooth them out and change to new pages to absorb the rest of the moisture. Replace the weight and let dry for several more days until the color is set and the material completely dry. Then store in firm boxes with moth crystals until ready to use.

The best kind of adhesive for mounting leaves is a milk-base glue such as Elmer's or Wilhold. I have found it adequate on a variety of surfaces—metal, wood, lacquer, and glass. It keeps the leaves soft and flexible while you are applying them. After the glue has dried you can brush the leaves with plastic lacquer or a coating of resin to bring up the colors and provide a protective layer for objects that are handled or subjected to liquids. These finishes also make it easier to keep objects dusted. (See Chapter 3, "Working with Resin," for instructions.)

Folding Screen
(Illustration 52)

Little screens from Japanese gift shops afford delightful decorating opportunities. You can also make your own screens of cardboard sections taped together and covered with paper. Spray them with gold or any other color. This particular screen has six panels, each 4 by 14 inches. It was originally a calendar and when it became

outdated I covered the twelve months with dark green veneer paper. With the neutral squares in between, this made a checkerboard background.

I selected pressed autumn leaves of red, gold, and russet shades of varied shapes, but allowed repetition to give rhythm and continuity to the design. Milk-base glue, spread with a brush over the back of each leaf, holds them in place. When dry, I covered the leaves with plastic lacquer. This brightens the colors and makes it easier to dust the screen. Illustration 56 shows another example.

Panel of Eucalyptus Leaves
(Illustration 53)

The bold simple shape and leathery look of eucalyptus leaves suggest contemporary designing. I collected the large leaves, mottled with bright green and red, in July, pressed them, and using milk-base glue, mounted them in an overlapping pattern on a board of masonite. To intensify their colors and provide a protective layer I

ILLUSTRATION 52

TABLE SCREEN. Individual leaves are displayed against squares of green and tan paper. This miniature 14-inch-high screen was once a Japanese calendar. *(Photo by Darrow M. Watt)*

poured on a thin coating of resin. Then I hung the panel from a small ring hanger fastened at the top over a textured strip of heavy, dark brown cork. Both are held flat against the wall by a thin nail through the ring and cork.

Autumn-leaf Tray
(Illustration 54)

Trays provide another surface suited to leaf montages. To decorate this wooden tray I began by gluing leaves at the edges, placing them to display the outline of the leaf rather then trimming the leaf to fit the edge. I filled in spaces with lentils, then proceeded to cover the rest of the tray, letting leaves overlap but showing as many complete leaves as possible. To bring out individual shapes I associated leaves of contrasting color. A rather thick layer of resin was poured over the collection to make the tray practical. With the addition of a flat

---

ILLUSTRATION 53

EUCALYPTUS LEAVES. Mottled green, red, and tan leaves are glued to a board of masonite and coated with resin, then mounted on a strip of dark brown cork. (*Photo by Darrow M. Watt*)

ring hanger on the back, this tray can also become an attractive wall decoration.

Orange Lacquer Trays
(Color Illustration 7)

Gay lacquered trays of all sizes and shapes can be handsomely embellished with leaves. You may have a few exceptionally lovely leaves you want to display individually or several well-matched pairs. Follow the general procedure outlined above using white glue and cover the inside of the tray with a coating of resin to protect the decoration.

Wastepaper Basket with Autumn Leaves
(Color Illustration 8)

To cover a surface that curves, as this wastepaper basket does, use flexible leaves without stems or stiff ribs. Milk-base glue keeps the leaves soft while you apply them. In this montage, leaves overlap to cover the surface completely. When the glue dried I poured resin

---

ILLUSTRATION 54

AUTUMN-LEAF TRAY. Overlapping leaves and a border of lentils decorate a tray which could also be a wall plaque. A coating of resin provides a waterproof surface. *(Photo by Darrow M. Watt)*

over the leaves, one side at a time, to make the basket practical to handle.

Windowpanes Covered with Leaves and Japanese Paper (Illustration 55)

For a window on the street or one that looks out on an unattractive view, pressed leaves, flowers, and butterflies combined with a delicate thin Japanese paper can be an enchanting means of achieving privacy with light. You may want to cover the window completely or just the lower half. Select very flat materials with no hard or rigid stems. I have used a porous, lacy Japanese paper called scatyoshino made translucent by the milk-base glue.

I suggest working out the placement of leaves and whatever else you plan to use on a flat surface about the same size as the window area before actually attaching the pieces to the window. Spaces between leaves and directions of stems are important parts of the design.

ILLUSTRATION 55

FOR PRIVACY. Pressed leaves, ferns, and butterflies with lacy Japanese paper provide an attractive design which lets light through. *(Photo by M. Van Rensselaer)*

When satisfied with the composition, glue the pieces to the glass using a milk-base glue (Elmer's or Wilhold).

Measure the Japanese paper to fit the windowpane exactly. If necessary the paper can be pieced with another sheet with overlapping torn edges. Mix up a solution of equal parts of the same milk-base glue and water. With soft, half-inch (or wider), blunt-end paintbrush apply a strip of glue solution to the top edge of the window and press the paper in place. Work downward, applying glue with wide strokes to the paper and pressing the paper flat. A narrow paint roller or a sponge roller from a stationery store, soaked in the glue solution, will help remove wrinkles. Any tears can be repaired with patches of paper with torn edges. A few wrinkles are inevitable. If after the paper is dry there are a few thin places, paint those spots with more glue solution.

Because water-based glue is used, you can remove the decoration from the window at any time.

For a Window Ledge
(Illustration 56)

A corner shelf of clear glass, mounted in grooves cut in a plain wooden two-sided frame, provides a surface of such simplicity that the form, color, and texture of the dried materials can be emphasized fully. Each piece was attached to the glass with white glue and pressed flat, then brushed with a plastic lacquer. (Natcol's Poly Coat, a resin you can apply with a brush, also works well.) Field grass outlines the curve of the glass. Lovely lavender and cream petals of the passion flower, combined with leaves of yellow ginkgo, red *Zelkova serrata,* autumn-brown oak, and a butterfly are arranged to be clearly seen.

Leaves and Flowers of Resin
(Illustration 57)

Exquisite translucent petals, leaves, buds, and flowers can be made with one of the thick resin compounds now available. Mrs. Carl Coate gave me this good idea and the procedure is quite simple. (See general directions in Chapter 3, "Working with Resin.") Select the natural materials you want to duplicate—they can be fresh or dried—mix resins and hardener and apply with a spatula or brush to the *back* of leaves or petals. Give at least two coats, letting each layer dry before applying the next. Then peel off the plant material. The delicacy and fine detail of the natural form is retained in the resin cast.

A combination I have used is equal parts of Fitz-E Sculpting Resin and Fitz-E Extra-Thick Clear Casting

Resin with about 3 drops of hardener to 1 heaping tea-spoon of each resin. You have to experiment with the amount of hardener you need. In hot weather I find I use less. Drying between applications is also affected by the temperature and amount of hardener.

A selection of leaves and flowers made of resin is shown photographed on purple stained glass which tinted the milky plastic in the picture. At the top left are three dark leaves, two magnolia and one ivy, with the leaves still on the resin forms. Below, resin petals of a magnolia blossom with a natural uncoated pod pressed into the resin while it was still soft. Top right, a fuchsia flower and two buds completely coated with resin and below them five fuchsia leaves. At the right of the mag-nolia blossom and lower left are darker veined magnolia leaves of resin, a warm russet color from the tomentum on the leaves. (Varieties of *Magnolia grandiflora* bear leaves with fuzzy rust-colored backs.) Lower center are two magnolia leaves of a different variety, and on the

---

ILLUSTRATION 56

Window Design. A quarter-circle of glass, edged with grass, and mounted in a two-sided frame provides an unusual way to dis-play dried leaves, a passion flower, and a butterfly. *(Photo by Darrow M. Watt)*

155

right, two ginkgo, two ivy, an osmanthus, and a liquid-ambar leaf.

Magnolia Blossoms and Leaves of Resin
(Color Illustration 16)

This plaque suggests one design for using resin leaves and flowers. To make this I removed nine magnolia petals from their stem. Using the combination of resins and hardener given above, I brushed on three coats to the backs of the petals and to the pod. When all were dry I attached a short heavy copper wire with additional resin to the end of each petal, and inserted these wires into holes drilled through the pod where the petals had been originally. I then trimmed the wires and made the petals firm with more resin applied to the back of the flower. The flower is glued to a sheet of orange-brown plexiglass. Four magnolia leaves of resin, rust-colored by the tomentum on the backs of the leaves, are also glued on.

With a T-square and razor-blade cutter I cut a block

ILLUSTRATION 57

RESIN LEAVES AND BLOSSOMS. Natural materials coated with a thick resin compound yield lovely translucent forms that keep the detail and design of the original flowers and leaves.

157

of inch-thick dark brown cork to 13 by 16 inches. Then, leaving a 2-inch frame, I cut out the center. I turned the frame over and cut away the back, retaining a narrow frame all around, and glued the plexiglass to the cut-out part.

Fuchsia Leaves of Resin with Glass Tubes for
Fresh Flowers
(Color Illustration 10)

This combination of resin leaves, glass tubes, and fresh flowers makes an unusual centerpiece or wall decoration. After making fifteen fuchsia resin leaves, according to the method described above, I attached a long, heavy copper wire to each leaf with a bit of resin compound. Starting at the top, I combined the wires into one stem, leaving a few inches of wire free to bend the stem into an attractive curve. To make the stems more decorative I wrapped wired gold braid around them.

Eight glass tubes are held in place with pale green chenille-covered wire. I wrapped one end of 12-inch sticks of chenille around the main stem and twisted the other end into coils to support the tubes.

There is a loop of wire on the back of this arrangement for hanging it on a wall, and the tubes can easily be bent upward to hold water.

158

Shown as a centerpiece, this arrangement was photographed on textured purple glass with dainty campanulas in the flower tubes.

Construction can easily be varied. The arrangement could be assembled with wire alone, leaving out the chenille-covered wire, and for a permanent decoration, dried flowers could be substituted.

Resin Petals on Plexiglass
(Color Illustration 12)

To make this colorful wall hanging I chose a narrow panel of quarter-inch-thick red plexiglass, 3½ inches wide and 21 inches long. The jewel-like red handsomely sets off the resin petals cast on stiff osmanthus leaves. (See preceding "Leaves and Flowers of Resin.") I used leaves of graded sizes to make the flower shapes and two eucalyptus caps, one inside the other, for flower centers. Each part is fastened to the plexiglass with clear glue.

After completing this stage I took the panel of plexiglass to a store to select the proper shade of felt, one that would relate to the color of the eucalyptus caps and also match the intensity of the red. A rich gold did both.

With a razor cutter and a steel ruler I cut a cardboard piece slightly larger than the plexiglass. Then, with **scissors,** I cut out the felt about half an inch larger than

159

the cardboard, pasted it to the cardboard (Higgins Vege-
table Glue works well), cut off the corners, turned the
edges over the cardboard, and glued them down. Just
to make the back neat I covered it with heavy brown
paper.

The plexiglass is attached to the felt with transparent
glue applied under the flowers. For hanging up the panel
I looped wire through two holes (made with an awl or
heavy needle) near the top of the cardboard.

7. Decorations from the Sea with Seaweed, Shells, Pebbles, and Glass

Craftsmen have only recently begun to explore ways to use such treasures as are found along the seashore. Lovely pebbles, bits of frosty glass, coarse and delicate sea plants, and shells of every shape and color all are there for the looking.

In this chapter I suggest ways to use seaweed and sea glass, stones, shells, and pebbles pretty much as they are found on the beaches. But hobby shops now offer sliced shells, rocks which have been sliced, polished, and tumbled, or even the equipment to do this yourself. Tumblers are inexpensive and the results exciting. Stones thus transformed can be made into bracelets, pins, earrings, and cuff links, or dangled on key chains.

Seaweed

The delicate patterns and unusual colors of seaweed are a delight to collectors. Along the water's edge at low

161

tide you are most likely to find interesting varieties, and little tide pools and coves among the rocks often contain unexpected treasures. When I go collecting I take along a coffee can with a lid to fill with ocean water. Even pieces which have dried can be softened in water. I keep the tightly sealed can or jar in the refrigerator until I am ready to press the seaweed or apply it wet. It will keep for several weeks.

How to Press Seaweed

I lay sprays of seaweed on waxed paper, and using drops of water, spread out the feathery parts with a small soft paintbrush. After each spray is displayed to full advantage, I tip the paper to drain off as much water as possible without disturbing the pieces. Then I put another sheet of waxed paper on top and place in a small press. If seaweed is thick I put a folded paper towel under the waxed paper and another paper towel on top before putting the seaweed into a press.

A little press is useful for both leaves and seaweed. I have one that has six boards, 12 by 7 inches, and an adjustable arm. It can be obtained through Gaylord Brothers in California (see listing in "Sources of Supplies").

After the seaweed has been in the press about 24 hours

I carefully remove the top sheet of waxed paper and lift the seaweed off the lower sheet. Then I lay it down again on two fresh sheets of waxed paper and put back in the press for another day or two. Delicate pieces are difficult to remove from the waxed paper when they are thoroughly dry; removing them when there is still a little moisture prevents damage.

Seaweed can also be pressed between pages of a telephone book with a weight on it. Change to new pages after the first day of pressing.

After a few days the seaweed is ready for mounting. I generally use white (milk-base) glue applied to the pieces with a thin knife or brush.

Decorative Screens
(Color Illustration 3)

A charming way to prolong enjoyment of delicate sprays of seaweed is to mount them on little screens covered with paper or sprayed with paint to provide a contrasting background. The screens illustrated are only 14 inches high and came from a Japanese gift shop.

I sprayed the paper-backed screen with several coats of Illbronze Super-Brite Gold to give it subtle texture and a sense of depth. Then I selected dainty pieces of deep red seaweed that had been pressed according to

163

directions above, and arranged them in each of the six panels. When I felt pleased with the overall design I applied white glue to the sprays with a thin knife blade and gently put them in place.

Seaweed-decorated Notepaper
(Illustration 58)

Katherine Kitchen of Tucson, Arizona, told me of this idea of applying tiny pieces of wet, unpressed seaweed to notepaper. You can use bond notepaper of medium weight or folded sheets of textured paper such as rice paper torn to fit into envelopes. (The ragged edge seems more appropriate to the rough papers.)

You will need on hand a shallow rectangular pan, paper toweling, waxed paper, round toothpicks, a small watercolor brush, tweezers, a pie pan of salt water, small scissors, and a press or stack of newspapers and boards with a heavy object for a weight.

Take the seaweed from the can in the refrigerator and float pieces in the pie pan while working. Cut a

---

ILLUSTRATION 58
SEAWEED-DECORATED NOTEPAPER. Delicate sprays of seaweed are applied to textured rice paper and smooth notepaper to make unusual stationery.

164

piece of waxed paper the size of notepaper to be decorated. Lay the waxed paper on a piece of glass or any
smooth surface that will not be damaged by water. With
tweezers lift seaweed from the pie pan, and after trimming it, arrange on the waxed paper.

Fill the rectangular pan with water. Submerge notepaper in it completely. Transfer the seaweed to the
notepaper, poking it into place with the toothpick or
brush. Lift the notepaper out of the water and let it
drain.

Put a fresh piece of waxed paper on the glass and lay
the decorated notepaper on it. Adjust any part of the
design with the brush and a small amount of water. Add
drops of water to the feathery parts to spread them out.
Lift waxed paper to drain off the water. Then remove
the notepaper from the waxed paper and place on a
folded paper towel on a smooth board. Put a sheet of
waxed paper on top. If the seaweed is extremely fragile,
a soft cloth is better. Lay a paper towel over the waxed
paper or cloth and place a board on top.

Proceed in this manner with the next sheet of notepaper. The following day remove the waxed paper carefully and replace both paper towels and waxed paper
and put between boards for three or four days until

completely dry. If there are any wrinkles in the note-paper they can be pressed out with a cool iron.

The soft seaweed becomes part of the paper. Stiff pieces may need a touch of glue after the design has been pressed and completely dried.

A Seaweed Picture with Starfish and Birds
(Illustration 59)

Treasures from the sea can be composed into three-dimensional pictures. For this one I selected a 5- by 13-inch redwood frame and attached a piece of trans-lucent fiberglass—the kind used for skylights—to the back of the frame with transparent glue. (The fiberglass is easily sawed or cut with heavy shears.) Shiny, dark brown seaweed from the deep sea, found on the beach near Dana Point in southern California, makes the tree. It is ornamented with starfish and red glass birds. At the base is a piece of brown bottle glass, slightly melted in a small electric kiln to soften the edges, and trimmed with a few tufts of red-brown volcano grass and a starfish. All pieces are attached with transparent glue. I poured a thin coat of resin over the entire picture since fiberglass is completely compatible with resin. (See "Working with Resin," Chapter 3.)

Shell Designs on Planters and Vases
(Illustration 60)

Another simple way to make decorative use of pretty shells is to attach them to planters, ceramics, vases, cups, and bowls. Depending on the delicacy and weight of the shells you can fasten them with transparent glue or ceramic-tile cement. Pressed seaweed (see preceding directions) can be glued on. Shells that have been sliced to display the inner structure make unusual decorations and are available from the Natcol Laboratories (see "Sources of Supply").

Sea Panel
(Color Illustration 2)

To make an interesting wall decoration of treasures from the sea, I arrange them first on a chosen background before putting them permanently in place. The

---

ILLUSTRATION 59
THREE-DIMENSIONAL PICTURE. Framed in redwood, this picture is made with shiny brown seaweed from deep water, starfish, red glass birds, brown volcano grass, and a piece of melted brown bottle glass. All are glued to a background of translucent fiberglass and covered with a thin layer of resin.

169

materials used for this sea panel are things I found on beaches and in hobby shops and garden shows. The frame is 4 inches deep, giving the effect of a shadow box. The background is a 16- by 38-inch piece of ribbed blue-green glass. After the arrangement was completed, and the pieces glued on, I poured several coats of resin over the entire composition to give it the quality of moving water. A few cracks developed in the glass because of the incompatibility between glass and resin when exposed to extreme cold. When working with glass backing it is better to pour resin only on the materials and not on the glass. Plexiglass makes an ideal surface for resin.

ILLUSTRATION 60

DECORATIVE PLANTERS. Shells and seaweed can be glued or cemented to plain vases and planters. At left, spirals of shells embellish an unglazed sand-colored planter. Sliced shells exhibiting interior design, whole shells, and pressed seaweed sprays are combined on the rough-textured turquoise ceramic in the center; the spiral shell at the rim hides a large chip. At right, small clam shells with purple stripes are applied with ceramic-tile cement to the rim of a deep blue vase.

Rattan Fish with Shells and Seaweed
(Illustration 61)

For these imaginative wall decorations on rattan frames Priscilla Blesch has used pieces from her fine collection of shells and seaweed. She first painted three of the frames with flat black, then scraped most of it off, to give a more definite outline to the fish shape but not an overpowering one. The lighter frame she painted a soft blue, then rubbed it with some of the blue-green dye with which the resin was to be tinted.

A large piece of mylar was used as a temporary backing. (See directions in "Rattan Frames and Resin," Chapter 3.) Mrs. Blesch applied transparent glue to the back of each frame and pressed it firmly to the mylar with a weight until the glue had set. Then she arranged the shells, sprays of pressed seaweed, and those with barnacles. Next she mixed the resin with hardener, tinted it with blue-green dye, and poured it over the arrange-

---

ILLUSTRATION 61
RATTAN FISH WITH SHELLS AND SEAWEED. Resin, tinted with blue-green dye, holds delicate shells and colorful seaweed in rattan frames. These fanciful wall decorations were created by Priscilla Blesch.

ment, immersing some materials and only coating others. When the resin was almost hard she removed the rattan frames from the mylar with a knife. The mylar can be set aside for the next project. Any resin that has seeped through to the outside of the frames can be trimmed with a paring knife at this stage. To hang the fish, she used fishline stretched between two tiny nails in the rattan.

Sea-glass Star
(Color Illustration 15)

Ocean-smoothed bits of glass, found at the edge of the waves often among drifts of pebbles, can become frosted jewels in the proper setting. Rattan frames offer innumerable possibilities. For this example I have used an 18-inch star and filled the center with a piece of mylar to have a backing for the glass. This method raises the glass pieces more effectively than gluing mylar to the back of the frame.

I first made a paper pattern of the center section and cut out a matching piece of mylar from the pattern. Because the frame is handmade and slightly irregular, I made guide marks on the mylar and frame so the mylar would fit exactly when put in place. Then I glued wired gold braid along the inside edges, wrapped it with fine

174

copper wire (which I removed when the glue was nearly dry), and turned the ends of the braid over the rattan in each corner. I sprayed the frame with Illbronze Super-Brite Gold and fitted the mylar into the center section, securing it to the braid with glue.

With translucent pieces of lavender, blue, turquoise, and white glass I made a design to fill the space, then attached the pieces to the mylar by spreading transparent glue on the back of each piece of glass.

I use this star as a wall ornament hung by a loop of wire over one of the rattan points. I found that the glass pieces needed color behind them to bring out their subtle beauty, and after trying several colors I settled on pink. Using the original pattern for the center section of the frame I cut out a piece of pink metal foil (the kind florists use around flower pots) and glued the edges to the back of the braid.

Picture of Glass Pieces
(Color Illustration 15)

A 6- by 9-inch piece of blue plexiglass is the backing for a picture I composed of glass pieces. The plexiglass is mounted on a sheet of spun aluminum to reflect light back through the glass bits and intensify their colors. I cut the aluminum slightly larger than the glass to have

175

enough to bend over the front for a narrow frame. To do this, slit the corners of the aluminum and bend the metal with the side of a heavy knife.

The glass pieces were sorted into colors and I glued them in place after deciding on the general elements of the picture. When completed I applied a 2-inch fabric hanger to the back of the aluminum.

Mobile for a Sunny Window
(Illustration 62)

Another way to display the frosty elegance of sea glass is to suspend the pieces by transparent lines and let them twist and turn in the sunlight.

To make mobiles you need small bell caps in silver or gold (they are found in hobby shops or can be ordered from Natcol Laboratories listed in "Sources of Supplies"); transparent fishline cut in lengths of one to two feet; snap swivels from a sporting-goods store; and an item of some kind from which to hang the glass.

In the mobile shown I used 24 pieces of amber, green, turquoise, and frosty white glass. They are hung from a Japanese teapot stand, a hexagonal, 6-inch mat made of golden bamboo sliced into hollow sections attached side by side. The mat is suspended by two pieces of gold chenille-covered wire, crossed and hung on a fisherman's

ILLUSTRATION 62

MOBILE OF SEA GLASS. Elegant frosted pieces of glass hang like
jewels from transparent lines looped over sections of a golden
bamboo mat.

177

snap swivel that is also hung by a length of gold chenille. The other end can be tacked to a shelf or bracket where the sun's rays will cast warm light on the translucent glass.

After devising the basic overhead construction, I shaped small gold or silver bell caps to the glass and glued them on. Then I tied one end of a length of fish-line, varying from one to two feet, to the ring on the bell cap, and put the other end through one of the holes in the bamboo, across the top and down through another hole. I decided on the length, then attached that end of the line to another piece of glass of about the same weight. You can adjust the pieces up and down until you have the best effect. This is the procedure for all pieces, with balance of size and color determining the relations.

Another of my mobiles is suspended from a Japanese mat of bamboo strips 6 inches long, woven together in two groups making staggered edges. I sprayed the brown bamboo a silver color to match the bell caps holding delicately colored glass. The mat is hung on four wires concealed between matched strips of silver rickrack braid, glued to the wire. Wires are hung on a snap swivel from a silver cord.

Rocks

A continuing source of enjoyment is rock collecting. Along the beach, a country road, by streams or mountain paths, water-smooth pebbles or rough chunky stones can be discovered. Some rocks suggest an outdoor setting. In our frontyard terraces I have developed a veritable mosaic of rocks, succulents, and driftwood. Other stones, particularly the smooth polished pebbles from beach or brook, are suited to decorating.

Planter with Rocks and Stones
(Illustration 63)

Stones, pebbles, and rocks can be used to decorate a planter, either those of one size and color, or an assortment, in an overall pattern or in rows or swirls. You can make designs with the planter as background or decorate with larger stones and fill in the background with small pebbles.

To enliven this unglazed sand-colored planter I selected a variety of smooth stones, sketched simple tree designs on the pot with a pencil and attached the stones with a waterproof ceramic-tile cement. The brand I have used here is slow drying and holds the rocks well, Garland-White CS/52. Flat sandstones make the top border

179

ILLUSTRATION 63

ROCK-DECORATED PLANTER. Sparkling flat gray rocks, small brown pebbles, and smooth shiny stones of many colors are attached to an unglazed planter with a waterproof ceramic-tile cement.

with larger colorful rocks below, while flat sparkling gray stones are the tree trunks. The branches are small, elongated brown pebbles, and the leaves are smooth shiny pebbles of rich coloration.

Pebbled Duplex for Birds
(Illustration 64)

This two-family birdhouse, partitioned down the center, is made of half-inch plywood and is 7 inches wide, 12 inches long, and 11 inches high. I selected flat, mottled, dark gray stones that sparkle for the roof and fitted them together like a puzzle before attaching them with ceramic-tile cement. Stones with straight sides made the edges. Once the stones were arranged I applied a drop of cement to each and pressed it firmly in place. A small pointed knife removes any cement that shows, and the recommended thinner solution for the cement can be used to wipe the knife clean.

The chimney is made of white pebbles fitted closely together. Flat tan sandstone covers the sides. On the edges of the roof and entrance platforms, and the roofs, I used smooth brightly colored pebbles found on the beach. Since the bottom of the house can be seen when it is up on the redwood post, I attached stones to it also. When completed, I painted the stones with resin (Nat-

181

col Poly Coat) to give the stones a shiny look and keep off the dust. The bracket on the bottom for attaching the house to the post was put on before the stones were attached.

ILLUSTRATION 64

BIRDHOUSE. This two-family wooden birdhouse is decorated with rocks and waterproofed with resin.

Sources of Supplies

Eucalyptus pods, 250 14th Ave., Santa Cruz, Calif. Kit of a large variety of small pods.

Eunice Curtis, 14407 S. E. 55th St., Bellevue, Wash. Pods from Africa and Australia.

Floral Art, P. O. Box 394, Highland Station, Springfield, Mass. A 30-page booklet for the flower arranger. Books, dry materials, and accessories.

Forni Sculpture, P. O. Box 2031, Santa Rosa, Calif. Stone sculpture of St. Francis and Madonna.

Jack Sullivan's, 1501 Broadway, Everett, Wash. Cones, pods, and dry materials.

Mountain Meadow Enterprises, Hotchkiss, Colo. Handcarved birds, desert grasses, and unusual cones in quantity orders for organizations.

Sierra Cone Shop, P. O. Box 117, El Portal, Calif. Western cones. *Sierra Cone News* published throughout the year with entertaining information for cone collectors.

St. Germaine's Flowers, P. O. Box 1795, Stockton, Calif. Dry materials, kits, and accessories.

The Fir Tree, P. O. Box 604, Mi-Wuk Village, Calif. Catalog of fine Sierra cones, a wide variety of pods and seeds for mosaics. Rack for wreath-making. Visit the shop if you are on Sonora Pass.

Treasures of the Sea and Land, 1458 State St., Schenectady, N. Y. Comprehensive list of dry materials, accessories, and do-it-yourself supplies.

PLASTIC SUPPLIES AND ACCESSORIES, SHELLS, AND POLY COAT

Natcol Laboratories, P. O. Box 299, Redlands, Calif. Two booklets describing the use of plastics. Comprehensive catalog of supplies.

PLASTICO ROK

Douglas and Sturgess, 730 Bryant St., San Francisco, Calif.

PRESS

Gaylord Bros., Inc., 29 Aurora St., Stockton, Calif. Small portable press for leaves and seaweed.

PROPYLENE GLYCOL FOR GLYCERINING LEAVES

The Wholesale Supply Company, 1005 Lillian Way, Los Angeles, Calif.

RATTAN FRAMES

Rattan N' Teak, 313 Town and Country Village, Steven's Creek Road, San Jose, Calif.

Barnett Hardware Co., 108 West Little Creek Road, Norfolk, Va.

VENEER WOOD, PLACECARDS, AND VENEER PAPER

Northgate Art, 349 N. Santa Cruz Ave., Los Gatos, Calif.

WIRE WREATH FRAMES

Mosser Lee, Millston, Wisc. Double wire frames for wreaths from 10 to 24 inches in diameter. Prepaid by the dozen.

Bibliography

Arnold Arboretum, *Bulletin of Popular Information* (Jamaica Plain, Mass.: Harvard University, December 16, 1955). Fresh wreath materials, dried fruits, flowers and cones from all parts of the United States.

Booke, Ruth Voorhees, *Pressed Flower Pictures* (Princeton, New Jersey: D. Van Nostrand Company, Inc., 1962). An enticing book for flower lovers, full of flower lore as well as a variety of projects for the craftsman.

Brooklyn Botanic Garden, *Handbook of Flower Arrangement* (Brooklyn, N. Y., 1955). Information on various phases of flower arrangement.

Casebolt, Florence Waye, *Button Gardens* (Alamo, Calif.: Button Garden Studio, 1440 Finley Lane, 1952). Instructions for making diminutive gardens with tiny flowers.

Collingwood, George C., *Knowing Your Trees* (Washington, D. C.: American Forestry Association, 1945). Trees and their leaves, bark, flowers, and fruit. 806 illustrations.

Cookson, Vangie, *Cone Creations* (Park Rapids, Minn.:

The Pine Cone Shop, Rt. 2). An attractive booklet with fresh new ideas, clearly described and well designed.

Hatton, Richard G., *Handbook of Plant and Floral Ornament from Early Herbals* (New York: Dover Publications, Inc., 1960). 1200 illustrations.

Lochry, Marie A., *Corsages of Pods and Cones* (Port Orchard, Wash., Box 114). Interesting combinations of materials. Well illustrated.

McMinn, Howard E., *An Illustrated Manual of Pacific Coast Trees* (Berkeley, Calif.: University of California Press, 1937). Descriptions of native Pacific Coast trees and about 400 introduced species. Leaves, cones, and pods well illustrated.

Riester, Dorothy, *Design for Flower Arrangers* (Princeton, New Jersey: D. Van Nostrand Company, Inc., 1955). A book to study carefully for design principles.

Sargent, Charles Sprague, *Manual of the Trees of North America* (New York: Dover Publications, Inc., 1922). Unabridged edition of the monumental work first published in 1905. Two paper bound volumes.

Seibel, Kathryn Holley, *Arts and Crafts for Flower Arrangers* (Princeton, New Jersey: D. Van Nostrand Company, Inc., 1961). A book filled with ideas for the craft minded, covering a wide range of projects clearly described and illustrated.

Sunset Western Garden Book (Menlo Park, Calif.: Lane Publishing Co., 1961). Comprehensive descriptions of all types of garden plants and their care.

Superintendent of Documents, *Forest Trees of the Pacific Slope* (Washington, D. C.: Government Printing Office, 1908). Native trees of the Pacific region with precise information on geographic range.

Van Rensselaer, Maunsell, *Trees of Santa Barbara* (Santa Barbara, Calif.: The Santa Barbara Botanic Garden, 1948). Illustrated guide to 745 species of trees, giving locations of over 1000 characteristic specimen trees.

Index

INDEX

INDEX

INDEX

196

INDEX

198